P9-EMP-723

# Better Groceries for Less Cash

## 101 _Tested_ & _Proven_ Ways to Save on Food

_By Randall Putala © 2009_

Copyright © 2008 by Randall Putala
All rights reserved

For information about permission to reproduce selections from this book, write to Permissions c/o SDMI, 5010 Linbar Drive, Suite 130, Nashville, TN 37211.

www.grocerysavings.us

Library of Congress Cataloging-in-Publication Data

Putala, Randall

Better Groceries for Less Cash / Randall Putala

ISBN 978-0-9777106-0-7.

Printed in the United States of America

Book design by John Hreha

# Contents

# Foreword

A man walks into a car dealership. He says to the salesman, *"I want to buy your finest vehicle and I'll pay the full sticker price, whether it is competitive or not. I don't care that the dealership down the street offers a lower price. I'm buying from you".*

The salesman looks stunned, but the man goes on: *"And don't even try to give me a better deal. No freebies or add-ons. I won't accept them. But I do want your sworn assurance that nobody – absolutely nobody – will pay more than me for the identical vehicle."*

The salesman recovers his wits and is delighted by his good fortune. Without blinking an eyelash now, he replies, *"my last customer took out a 5 year extended warranty. I'm assuming that you'll want the 10 year warranty, correct?"*

If you're thinking this scenario is a little farfetched, of course you're correct. But as you'll see in the pages of this book, it's not that far removed from the everyday reality that most people experience in their grocery store. And based on the way most people view food shopping, it's not really as absurd as you might think.

That's because most people view food shopping as an entirely different process than shopping for other items – especially high-ticket items.

Most people pride themselves on getting the absolute best deal on a new car, concocting elaborate schemes to 'work the sales person down'. They'll print out comparison reports from the internet, call every dealership in a 50 mile radius – heck, they'll even threaten to walk out of the dealership if they don't get the concessions they want. All this, for a purchase made once every five or six years that immediately loses about 10% of its value when you drive it off the lot.

Yet these very same consumers who spend countless hours scheming and negotiating to get the best deal on their new car, probably never stop to scrutinize the details of their grocery receipts. Are groceries the new "high ticket items" of our current economy? Just look at your receipts, and you'll get the answer immediately. Welcome to the bizarre world of economics 101.

You see, a new car can last you many years with a bit of regular maintenance. And at the end of the day, it's pretty much a one-time investment. But groceries are bought _every single week_ of _every single year._ They represent 15% to 20% of most household budgets, yet most people are PROUD to pay full price for everything from produce to pizza pies to polka-dot party plates. Does this make any sense to anybody???

Imagine the headlines if we had 'truth in advertising' and the grocery stores were forced to follow it: "Nobody Soaks You Better", "You'll Pay More – And LIKE It", or "Why Pay Less When We Can Charge You More?"

Of course, I'm being facetious. But the same people who will drive 5 miles out of their way to save a nickel on gasoline, will shudder at the thought of clipping grocery coupons. "I'm not poor!" they insist, as if they couldn't use an extra $1,000 or more per year. Sure, if your money grows on trees or you discover the secret of alchemy, you probably don't need to clip coupons. It's no big deal for someone like that to dismiss the $40,000 or $50,000 in savings they could enjoy over the course of their life. They can ridicule the coupon-clippers and laugh that they tip more than that to the valet parkers at their country club. Is this you? Do you light your cigars with $100 bills? Do you consider yourself the equal of the guy in the 'Monopoly" game with the monocle and the bow tie? If so, put this book down immediately and go count your Krugerrands!

I'm guessing, perhaps, that you're NOT that guy. Just maybe you don't carry a money clip with a wad of $100 bills, and just maybe you would enjoy saving $100 or $200 per month. If so, take a deep breath and relax: _this book is for you_, and _I really can show you how to do it_.

I really will show you how to enjoy savings of 30% - 40% – even 50% off your grocery bill, like clockwork, week in and week out. Read, enjoy, and happy savings!

Randall Putala
Author

P.S.    I've listed my "101 Big Ideas" at the end of each chapter to summarize the key points; refer to these time and again for a quick 'refresher course' to help you save money throughout your lifetime. If you find yourself drifting back into old habits, just breeze through the "101 Big Ideas" to remember how to get back on track.

# Chapter 1: What Color is Your Shopping Cart?

Before we discuss ways to save money at the grocery store, let's determine what type of grocery shopper you are at present.

Which of the following grocery shoppers best describes you?

**1. OUT OF MY WAY, I'M IN A HURRY.** I'm too busy, I've got a family to feed, just give me the makings of a quick meal and I'm out of here. I'd like to save money, but it's just not possible with my schedule.

**2. I'M CHOOSY. LET ME COMPARE.** Time is not as important to me as saving money. Let me compare the prices of each item on the shelf, and pick the cheapest one.

**3. I'M IN A HURRY, AND I'M CHOOSY.** Let me grab the highest-quality items on the shelf (based on brand name, advertising campaign, highest price, or position on the shelf). Let me grab the most expensive fruits and vegetables and the most expensive pre-cooked items at the deli counter. I want the best for my family and I'll buy it even if I can't afford it. I can find some other area of my life to cut costs – maybe.

**4. I'M LOST. JUST GIVE ME SOMETHING TO EAT.** I'll buy whatever is in front of me or whatever catches my eye today. I may end up with all the wrong stuff and I'm not sure if I'm getting a good deal, but at least I'm bringing home something edible.

**5. I'M IN A HURRY, I WANT THE BEST STUFF, AND I'M FRUGAL.** I've planned out my shopping trip to cut my in-store time to a minimum. I've reviewed my store's sales flyer in advance and selected the special deals and coupons I'm going to use. I'm going to select the finest core ingredients and plan my meals as I go based on the best deals I find in my store today. I'll be out of here in no time, I'll save 30% or more on my groceries, I'll easily pay only a **FRACTION** of what most others pay and my family will probably be eating better and healthier food than theirs.

*Wouldn't you like to be in that final group?*

Welcome to the first meeting of "Grocery Shoppers Anonymous", a first-names-only group for people who habitually pay too much for their groceries. It's a very good sign that you're willing to attend today's meeting, because this means you've acknowledged the problem and are willing to take action to change it.

Here, our therapy starts with the MINDSET you carry with you into the store.

The MINDSET you bring into the grocery store is what determines the amount you will pay for your food. You CANNOT CONTROL the prices that the grocery store charges you. But you CAN CONTROL your mindset about the items you will need to prepare your meals and hence you CAN CONTROL the items you put into your cart. Change your mindset, and you will lower your food costs. It's that simple.

If that paragraph didn't resound like a fire alarm in your brain, please read it again. It's very important. So do it. Now.

## Big Idea Recap – Chapter 1

*BIG IDEA 1: The MINDSET you bring with you into the grocery store is what determines the amount you will pay for your food. Change your mindset, and you'll lower your food costs. It's that simple.*

# Chapter 2: The "7 Deadly Sins"

*(Signs that you may be losing the "grocery game")*

1.       **High grocery expenses.** Keep your receipts for one month. Add up the total of all your grocery purchases. What percent of your family's take-home monthly income is going towards food? Is it reasonable, or is it OUT OF CONTROL?

2.       **Insufficient food supply.** If you often find one of your kids standing in front of the refrigerator shouting, "there's nothing to eat", you're probably suffering from an insufficient food supply. This is also known as spending too much on not enough. A budgeting problem is hardly ever managed by reducing the AMOUNT of food you bring home. A strategy like this does not make for happy campers and is rarely sustainable.

3.       **Unhappy campers.** Does your family ever politely suggest that your menu choices somehow fail to live up to their expectations? (Or perhaps they throw their full plates into the sink and yell "this food #*!)@"</&#s!"). If this is the case, you probably have a troupe of unhappy campers and it's your job as the conscientious and devoted parent you are to address this problem.

4.       **Uneaten goods.** If the food that you thought you needed is still in your fridge, freezer, or pantry months after the fact, you may not be making smart choices for your family. Everyone is different, and everyone likes different things from time to time. Are you experiencing these symptoms?
   a. You never seem to get around to cooking the items you purchase, and they sometimes go bad before you realize it.
   b. You get significant complaints whenever you serve the items you purchase.
   c. You have items that you never seem to run out of.
   d. Conversely, you have items that disappear as soon as you bring them home.

If any of these symptoms apply to the food situation in your home, they're a good indication that you are purchasing the wrong items – or the wrong quantities of items – for your family's needs.

**5.     Excessive leftovers.** Do you routinely throw a significant amount of food in the trash or down the drain? This means one of two things:
    a. You're cooking too much food. Your cooking proportions are too large, or you're making too many different dishes during a given time frame.
    b. You're cooking the wrong stuff. Your family just isn't "into" to the food you're cooking.

**6.     Binge snacking.** Are frequent snacks replacing meal times in your household? Do your kids skip the meals you cook only to wolf down an entire bag of chips at midnight? Eating the wrong kinds of food – at the wrong times – in the wrong quantities – can very quickly translate into serious health problems. It's important to correct this type of eating disorder early-on – and this book can help you.

**7.     Sticker shock.** Have you ever come home from the grocery store and really looked at your receipt? I mean more than just glancing at it – I mean reading it line for line, item by item. Sometimes the items that looked so good at the store cause palpitations when you see what you actually paid for them. Your significant other might even weigh in with their opinion, *"how could you pay $X for THAT?"* You probably don't want to admit that you didn't check the price in the first place. It just looked good at the time, so you put it in your cart. You may not even know WHY you put it in your cart. But something made you want to take that action, so you did. (More on this subject later in the book; keep reading.)

The primary job of grocery store marketers is to make you believe that you NEED their product to adequately feed and appease your family. There is a HUGE disconnect between this premise and the reality of the situation, but few people notice it. You can adequately feed a family of 5 for a few dollars if you select the right foods and recipes. The TV commercials you watch and the magazine ads you read are designed by food manufacturers to steer you away from cooking fresh foods and steer you toward buying their the high-priced pre-mixed concoctions. Steer yourself back to the basics, and your budget will thank you for it.

## Big Idea Recap – Chapter 2

*BIG IDEA 2:* *Grocery prices are rising faster than just about any other commodity in your life. Is your income rising to keep pace? If not, you either have to sacrifice some of the things you currently enjoy, or find a way to buy more for less. The second choice may seem a little painful at first, but remember that in today's economy you're going to have to work harder JUST TO STAY EVEN.*

*BIG IDEA 3:* *Your family is not going to be willing to eat LESS. If you can learn a few simple techniques to stretch your food budget and allow them to eat BETTER, you'll all be happier and healthier.*

*BIG IDEA 4:* *If your garbage disposal consumes more food than your family, it doesn't matter what you're buying or what you're cooking: something is significantly wrong in your relationship with food.*

*BIG IDEA 5:* *The TV commercials you watch, the print ads in your magazines, and even the signs in the grocery store, are all geared toward getting you to FORGET about cooking fresh and rely on pre-mixed, pre-bagged, pre-cooked, expensive meals. Re-program your brain to ignore these messages and rely on your own common sense to buy core ingredients instead.*

# Chapter 3: Here's Your Sign

Let's take a closer look at each of the 5 classic shopper types, and how grocery store owners attempt to extract the most possible cash out of each of your wallets – i.e. how each of you may be losing "the grocery game."

**1. "OUT OF MY WAY, I'M IN A HURRY".** You just got off work. Latchkey kid #1 is at his friend's house waiting for you to get home. Sports jock kid #2 is due back from baseball practice in 45 minutes. Workaholic hubby gets home in about an hour. All three are expecting a good dinner, meticulously prepared by tender, loving you. Your approach: "GET OUT OF MY WAY, GALS, OR I'LL MOW YOU DOWN!" You're zooming through the aisles snagging boxes and cans of anything that looks fast and edible that will pacify the hungry mob at home. Saving money on groceries is just about the furthest thing on your mind. Until you balance the checkbook later that week. Uh-oh. *"How did we spend $900 on groceries last month? That's UN-BEE-LEEVABLE! What, do you not check the prices? Don't you ever buy things on sale?"* Here are some tips exclusively for this shopper type:

**a.       BLOCK IT.** Create a 'block' of recipes and ingredients that you can fall back on. I recommend buying a small pocket-sized spiral book. Write down the simple recipes for meals you know your family will eat. List the ingredients you'll need. Divide this notebook into 6 sections and highlight the bottom with a marker to create visual tabs for quick reference:

*i.       Main Courses.* List the simple things your family will eat like Sloppy Joes, Hamburgers, Casserole, Chicken Fingers, etc.

*ii.       Side Dishes.* List things like Macaroni & Cheese, Baked Potatoes, Vegetable Medley, Au Gratin Potatoes, etc.

*iii.       Snacks.* List simple recipes you can make to pacify the hungry mob at odd hours of the day, things like Caramel Corn, Potato Skins, Nachos, Sandwiches, Fruit Salads, etc.

**b.** **REPLACE IT.** Use these blocks of recipes to purchase core ingredients at the store, INSTEAD of the bags of pre-mixed / pre-cooked items you've been buying. As you build your list of substitute recipes, you'll slowly wean yourself away from buying the higher-priced items. Add to your list of recipes by browsing the web. Buy some cheap cookbooks at yard sales, or check some out from the library. Keep adding to your list of recipes. If the family hates it, tear the sheet out of your notebook. If they love it, put a star by it.

The more you document your cooking successes and failures, the more you'll save. By writing down the things you learn in the kitchen – whether from a recipe, a book, or simple experimentation – the more you'll learn about how to both please your family with better recipes, and save on the ingredients that make up those recipes. You cannot rely on your memory to remember 'how you did it last time', but you *can* rely on your own notes.

**2. I'M CHOOSY. LET ME COMPARE.** If you're a slow and steady shopper but you just can't seem to save money, this description fits you to a T. You compare prices closely: The name-brand item is 99¢, and the off-brand is 89¢. So you buy the off-brand, thinking you're saving money. <u>*Not necessarily!*</u> If you had clipped a coupon from the Sunday paper for 25¢ off the name-brand item, your grocer would have doubled it, saving you 50¢ on the name-brand item. Final cost = 49¢ for the name-brand item vs. 89¢ for the off-brand item. You would have just reduced your cost of that item by almost 45%! Suggestions for this category of shopper:

**a.** **CLIP IT.** Clip coupons for every conceivable item you might buy at the store. You're already good at comparing prices. Factor in the power of coupons; it can really impact your budget.

**b.** **COMPARE IT.** If you're good at reviewing ingredients, compare the cost of buying the fresh ingredients vs. buying the pre-mixed items. For example, if you like the convenience of frozen bagged dinners, consider buying larger portions of each key ingredient, and then chopping down and bagging your OWN version of the pre-mixed dinners. You can prepare 5 or 10 meals in a single afternoon, and lower your cost of each meal by 50% or more!

**3.    I'M IN A HURRY, AND I'M CHOOSY.** This type of shopper is both finicky and non-frugal. You're the grocery manager's dream customer. They place the most expensive and appealing items at the end caps of the aisles and in the aisle bins, knowing you'll like the look of these particular selections and won't consider the alternatives or the lower-priced items. You are perhaps the hardest nut to crack in the grocery savings game. The best advice I can give you is as follows:

**a.    PORTION CONTROL.** Continue to buy the premium ready-made foods your family loves; just buy less of it. Make all-natural side dishes to add depth to your meal, while reducing costs.

**b.    MEAL FILLERS.** Add items to your menu that are fast, easy, and economical to cook. Put these on the plate along with smaller portions of the premium foods. This way your family fills up on healthy foods – just not the most expensive healthy foods. For example, let's say you typically bring home about $50 worth of Sushi to make a quick dinner for your crew. Try buying $15 worth of Sushi, but add side dishes such as rice with gravy, rice cakes topped with cream cheese and a small dollop of caviar *(see, you can upgrade and still save money!)* Or how about some celery pieces filled with tuna fish salad on the side? If you're creative, you can fill out the plate with lower-cost items that complement your original menu choices just fine.

**c.    CHANGE THE SOURCE OF THE SAME FOOD YOU SERVE.** For example, if you buy take-out Chinese once a week and spend $50 on one meal, consider buying $10 worth of Chinese food and adding some side dishes that you cook at home. One food manufacturer, everyone's favorite uncle, makes a fast-cooking pre-seasoned rice mix in foil pouches. There are always 2-for-1 deals at the store, and frequently there are coupons for this item in the Sunday paper. It means that you can get real deals on this product. It's fast to cook, and it's delicious. Plus, you'll end up paying 25¢ or so per portion vs. $2.00 per portion for rice from the Chinese take-out place.

___You don't have to give up the fine foods you know and love.___ To save money, simply buy less of the premium meal items and prepare value-based side dishes to supplement the main food selections. If you plan these side dishes carefully, the variety will make your meals healthier and enhance your main items as well.

## 4. I'M LOST. JUST GIVE ME SOMETHING TO EAT.

If you are this type of shopper, you should be pretty open to new suggestions. Chances are you feel pretty hopeless when it's time to grocery shop. Rest assured, though, all is not lost. You're really more of an open slate and one of the easiest to set on the right course. If you actually enjoy wandering around the grocery store like a lost helium balloon, you may have a problem. The best bets to get you on a more logical course in your grocery store visits are:

**a.     START SMALL.** Take really, really, REALLY, small steps to organize your shopping trips. Make a simple list by category, writing down how many items you'll need that week from each category. Keep it simple, like "3 meat items", "5 breakfast items", etc. If you can find coupons in the Sunday paper for some of the things you like, clip them out and put them in an envelope. Try to get to the point that you're reaching your goal of the number of items in each category, and stop there. Containment is the key word here, closely followed by completion of your assigned task.

**b.     MASTER SOME SIMPLE FOOD ITEMS.** Work on learning to cook individual items really well, and keep a small spiral binder to note down what you've learned. Be specific and write down the things you did that worked, as well as the things you did that DIDN'T work. For example, if you're trying to bake a potato in your microwave, write down the steps:

i.      *Poke holes in potato with fork*
ii.     *Wet the potato with running water*
iii.    *Sprinkle it with sea salt*
iv.     *Cook for 5 minutes on high.*

If this works, great. If you need more time, change it to 7 minutes, 8 minutes, etc. until you get it absolutely right. You now have detailed notes that you can read anytime you plan to make a baked potato. Next, try cooking 2 potatoes at once, and write down notes for this. As you master each new step, you're building your own cookbook of things that you know you can cook, that will turn out perfectly. Isn't that a great feeling?

Trial and error in the kitchen can be a valuable thing and it will help you determine what works for you. You'll waste a lot of food and put up with unhappy diners every now and again – but use recipes and cook books to help get you 'in the ballpark'. Watch the cooking shows on TV to see how professional chefs do things. The reason it looks so effortless on TV is because cooking is really very simple. It just takes practice to know what works, and then doing those same things next time you cook.

**5.     I'M IN A HURRY, I WANT THE BEST STUFF, AND I'M CHEAP.** If you mentally prepare yourself to reach this level, you're ready for the master class. The tips and techniques outlined in this book will be like manna in the desert: you're ready to shop. Imagine being able to wheel your cart out of the supermarket, chock full of the finest foods in the store. The checkout clerk and bag boy were amazed at how little you paid for so much food. The guy in line behind you, while kind of ticked off at how long the cashier took to scan all of your coupons, was fascinated watching the 'amount due' total going down, down, down, down. When your 'total savings' amount is $50, $60, $70 or more – and his 'total savings' amount is $2.27 – he's kind of wondering what you did. You can experience this every week – year-in and year-out – so you are literally saving $2,500 – $3,000 – $3,500 or more per year on groceries. Since these are 'after tax' savings – it is like getting a $5,000 raise at work.

**Get cheap, and stay cheap.** Approach the grocery store with a mission in mind: to show the maximum amount of savings on your receipt at the end of the trip. It will make you think about each of your selections and how they will affect your total. Some items will be necessities, and you won't always have a coupon for them or an alternative lower-cost option. But with at least 70% of your shopping cart items, you CAN do better if you just review your options.

## Big Idea Recap – Chapter 3

*BIG IDEA 6: The more you document, the more you'll save. By writing down the things you learn in the kitchen – whether by recipe, book, or simple trial & error – the more you'll learn about how to both please your family* with better recipes, and save on the ingredients that make up those recipes. You cannot rely on your memory to remember 'how you did it last time', but you can rely on your own notes.

**BIG IDEA 7:** *Want the convenience of 'single bag / single pan' cooking? Mix your own freezer bags full of core ingredients in advance, and you can prepare an entire month's worth of meals in a single afternoon.*

**BIG IDEA 8:** *You don't have to give up on the fine foods your family craves. To save money, simply buy less of them and prepare value-based side dishes to supplement your main food selections. If you plan these side dishes carefully, the variety will make your meals healthier and enhance the enjoyment of your main items.*

**BIG IDEA 9:** *Trial and error in the kitchen can be a valuable thing and help you determine what works for you. But you'll waste a lot of food and have unhappy and unfed diners who won't appreciate your efforts. Use recipes and cook books to help get you 'in the ballpark' of cooking success before you get started. Watch the cooking shows on TV to see how they do things. The reason it looks so effortless to them, is because cooking is really very simple. Learn what works for you, and document it so you can continue to build on your simple successes in the kitchen.*

**BIG IDEA 10:** *Get cheap, and stay cheap. Approach the grocery store with a mission in mind: to show the maximum amount of savings on your receipt at the end of the trip. It will make you think about each one of your selections and how they will affect your total. Some items will be necessities, and you won't always have a coupon for it, or an alternative lower-cost selection to make. But with at least 70% of your shopping cart items, you CAN do better if you just review your options.*

# Chapter 4: The "12 Steps to Recovery"

If you are a candidate for "Grocery Shoppers Anonymous", here is a list of the 12 steps on the road to recovery *(with my apologies to every real 12-step program out there...)*

**Step 1 – Acknowledge.** You must first of all admit that you need help cutting your grocery costs. If you don't think you have a problem (or won't admit it) you won't get anywhere.

**Step 2 – Believe.** Your second step on the road to recovery involves believe that you actually can pay less for your groceries. If you're currently paying $200 per week, visualize yourself paying $100. Change is all about visualization at this early stage.

**Step 3 – Be Flexible.** Once you can visualize the change you want, you've got to be prepared to try new things. You don't have to eat foods you don't like but you've at least got to try out new things once in a while. If you do what you've always done, you tend to get what you've always gotten.

**Step 4 – Reflect.** Take a close look at your mental relationship with food and your family's groceries. What is REALLY going on here...? How do you really feel about food? Examine your motives for buying the types of food you buy, and what they are doing to your health, your mental attitude, and your weight. If you don't understand why you do the things you do, write down the individual items that you think are causing the problem. Write down how they make you feel, and what experiences in the past are causing you to make these purchases over and over again. If you still don't understand the connection, seek professional counseling. Seriously. It can be a big help.

**Step 5 – Affirm.** Once you've taken a closer look at your groceries, you're probably going to be aware that some of the items that regularly appear in your shopping cart are perhaps not the best choices. Stand by this realization. Make yourself accept it.

**Step 6 – Reconsider.** Once you've uncovered the current negatives regarding your shopping habits, it's time to look at the positive solutions before you. Be open to the idea of putting **new** items in your shopping cart.

**Step 7 – Be Humble.** Humilty is the stepstone of success. When you reach for that high-priced non-essential food item, your mind may think of it as a reward. You may be thinking, *"I've always eaten this, I've always been able to afford it, I'm entitled to this and no one can stop me from buying it."* When your conscious mind says this to your subconscious, you must mentally shout out, **"STOP!"** Reset your mind, and enter a new instruction, *"I can make a better choice that will become my NEW favorite, for the NEW me."* Find a substitute, buy it, and if you like it – keep buying it.

**Step 8 – Record.** Take a notepad and physically stand in front of your pantry, your refrigerator and your freezer. Write down every item that you probably shouldn't have purchased, items that cost too much, or items that could be replaced with lower-cost selections. These are the "bad guys" that are eating a hole in your budget…

**Step 9 – Substitute.** Now comes the fun part. There's a lot for you to learn about food. Even the best chefs learn something new every day. Start experimenting with new ingredients and recipes. Find new ways of doing things that work for you and your family. Consider using lower-priced or healthier ingredients in your favorite recipes. Examples: plain yogurt instead of sour cream; cholesterol-lowering spread instead of butter, tofu instead of cheese.

**Step 10 – Reject.** When you have finished going down an aisle in the grocery store, review the items that you picked up in that aisle. Were they of the best value? Did you check to see if you had coupons for the items you selected? Did you consider other brands that might have been priced lower and been just as good? If not, turn around, put the guilty items back on the shelf, and 'do the aisle again.'

**Step 11 – Baby Steps.** Acknowledge that you cannot remake yourself or your dietary selections overnight. Too much change will cause rejection and abandonment of the whole project. Take it slow.

**Step 12 – Rejoice.** Reward yourself for taking specific steps to lower your food costs. If you saved $20 – put a $20 bill in your piggy back for a rainy day or a splurge event later in the year. If you're very diligent, get 'cash back' equal to that amount, and put it in a bank savings account immediately. You can open one at the in-store bank that most grocery stores have these days.

# Chapter 5: The Myths & Misconceptions of Store Coupons

The core of any grocery savings plan is store coupons. Love them or hate them, it doesn't matter. They're the number one promotional device in the grocery industry and you're going to have to come to terms with them. People tend to have fixed opinions about grocery coupons, and – unfortunately for their budgets – most of them are wrong. Let's examine the top 10 myths about store coupons; see if you can find your opinions among these common shibboleths.

**MYTH 1: Only poor people use coupons.**

**REALITY:** Only <u>smart</u> people use coupons. Imagine that you are at a social function where door prizes are being given away. Imagine your name is drawn from a hat and the prize is a brand-new $50 bill. Would you turn it down, on the basis that you already earn a salary and don't really need the $50? Would you return it and ask that it be given to a poorer person – someone who could "really use it"? Of course not! It's found cash, and it's your lucky day. You'd snatch up the $50 and celebrate winning a valuable prize.

Why then do people turn down $50 to $75, even $100 or more in savings on groceries? By not clipping and using store coupons, you're turning down the chance to save a ton of money. When I go shopping, if I save $50 on my weekly groceries, I feel disappointed; I know that I probably could have saved a lot more if I had shopped correctly!

By the way, Oprah Winfrey uses coupons. She's not exactly poor... Smart, yes – but not poor. In fact, the richest people in the world tend to be incredibly frugal... believe it or not, knowing how to value money is really what made them rich in the first place. The richest people in the world don't go around flashing money. They are always looking for ways to save, save, save! Knowing the value of money is the first step to keeping and building even more money in the future. Respect what you have been given and treat it properly, and more will be given to you over time.

**MYTH 2: If you can afford to pay full price, using coupons is a waste of time.**

**REALITY:** If your _spare_ time is worth more than $100 per hour, you're probably better off hiring someone to do your grocery shopping, let alone shopping for yourself, let alone using coupons. When you arrive at this conclusion, and "oh so many" of today's ultra-successful Hummer-driving success stories make this conclusion, be sure you're talking about your SPARE time. By this I mean the actual cash you would be generating in your spare time, and not the billing rate you would command if you were in the office.

If your spare time is exactly the same as your work time, and you really do work every moment of every day, remember Jack: all work / no play... it doesn't have a happy ending. You probably deserve a break, so take one.

Even if you're making tons and tons of money during your work time, just imagine for a moment what you and your family could do with an extra $2,000 or $3,000 per year. I'm talking about totally fun money... money that you can use to do anything you want... money to blow on a super vacation, a new hot tub, a monster home entertainment system ...whatever you consider TOTALLY FRIVOLOUS and TOTALLY DESIRABLE. Would you give less than an hour of your time each week to get it? Would you actually stoop to getting out a pair of scissors and clipping coupons to get it? If not, why not just go back to the office for another hour each week? Would that be easier?

Folks, here is a **huge** lesson that you can learn now or learn later: **SAVING money is the same thing as EARNING money.**

If you have an easy way to 'turn on the tap' to put more money in your pocket, you're very lucky. But if you're like the 99% of us who have to live on a fixed income or a regular paycheck, consider opening your mind up to ways that can SAVE your money so you can do more with what you've got.

"A penny saved is a penny earned." Benjamin Franklin said it, not me. And now his picture is on the $100 bill...!

Here's another way to look at wealth and financial status. If you truly feel you do not need to save on groceries, tell me this: do you have any credit card debt? If you owe ANY creditor ANY amount of cash, you're written in that creditor's shylock book. "Oh, no" you might say, "I don't deal with a shylock or a gangster, my credit card is with one of America's premier banking institutions." Okay, great. View it however you like. You're still on a pay-as-you-go plan, one that will take an immense amount of financial change to dig your way out of. "Vinnie" the shylock won't be driving by to break your knee caps. Instead, "Vincent" from the bank will simply break your credit score until you cough up the "vig" – 21%+ interest on the balance due. Same criminals / same effect: the situation has just been prettied-up to make you feel better about it.

Picture it this way: saving on your groceries can be a valid way to help you pay off your debt faster. It's not rocket science. You'll have more money set aside at the end of the month and that can go towards your debt.

**MYTH 3: You end up paying about the same, even if you use coupons.**

**REALITY:** Effective couponers can literally cut their food cost in half without even trying. It means that instead of writing a check for $150 for groceries, you write a check for $75. That's real money, and it really does stay in your bank account. If you use coupons effectively, along with the other techniques described in this book, you will end up paying less in hard cash at the grocery checkout. That is a fact.

If you write smaller checks to your grocery store, you'll have more money left in your checking account at the end of the day. Trust me, it's a nice feeling!

**MYTH 4: Grocery coupons are just a come-on to get you to buy overpriced items or "weird" items you really don't need.**

**REALITY:** Grocery coupons are issued for hundreds of everyday items – things you already buy for your family. Yes, many of them are for new items that you may not want or need. Some are also for products that are overpriced. But guess what? If you don't want it, don't need it, or don't like it, *don't buy it!* There are hundreds of other coupons available for items your family really does want, need and use every day. Use the coupons you need and don't use the ones you don't. You shouldn't use coupons as an excuse to buy things you don't need. You'd be ignoring the other principles we discuss in this book about planning your shopping list before you head out the door and really thinking about what your family wants and needs.

Just remember this: all grocery products were new at some point in time. You've been buying your favorites your whole life. Maybe you'll find some new favorites if you just try them one time.

**MYTH 5: People will think I'm destitute if I use coupons.**

**REALITY:** If you truly are independently wealthy, you probably don't need to use coupons. But I don't know of a single family who would turn down a free weekend in the Bahamas or at Disney World. I don't know of a single person who would say "no" to getting a free new wardrobe every year, or a free trip to Paris including hotel and airfare. Would you turn these things down if they were offered to you? I didn't think so...

If you can <u>already afford</u> these things every year without putting a dent in your budget, or you simply don't want the nicer things in life, you're right: maintain your affluent / happy / free-wheeling image, and don't use coupons. However, if you *don't* regularly treat yourself and your family to items like these, the techniques described in this book provide a real opportunity for you to start doing so. Then, when you're jetting across the Atlantic with a glass of Chardonnay in your hand, picture the people who make you feel destitute in the grocery store: are they on the plane with you? When you're headed to Paris to spend the money you've saved, will you care what those nay-sayers think? I didn't think so...

**Smart money management never goes out of style.** But weak money management can seriously cramp your style. Maybe not today but certainly later in life. Pennies that you save today will compound into dollars over time. Small debt that you start to rack up today will compound into larger debt over time, and that can be very hard to overcome. The moral of this story: saving pennies leads to saving dollars. Saving dollars early in life will lead to a much more robust lifestyle in your future. Let the mockers laugh: you're building for your future, not theirs.

**MYTH 6: It's unethical to use coupons if I can afford to pay full price.**

**REALITY:** Grocery manufacturers WANT you to use their coupons. They don't pay tens of thousands of dollars to distribute them in the hope that nobody will use them. Couponing is the #1 PROMOTIONAL TOOL available to the grocery industry. Manufacturers issue coupons according to a well-structured plan to build market share in specific parts of the country. If they didn't want consumers to buy their products, they wouldn't issue the coupons. In fact, the higher the coupon redemption rate, the more products they sell. They must replenish the sold product, so this increases jobs for the people at the factory, and increases sales for the farmers and food producers. Coupons help spur the economy, regardless of who redeems them.

Eva Peron insisted that Argentina should not cry for her (despite being an enormously popular public figure and despite dying young… see the movie "Evita" for details). If you're crying for the Fortune 500-listed grocery manufacturers, you *really do* have too much time or money on your hands…

**MYTH 7: Grocers do not want affluent shoppers to use coupons.**

**REALITY:** Who spends the most at grocery stores? It's the affluent households who can afford the more 'frivolous' products: pre-mixed items, super-premium items, higher-priced items, etc. The grocery manufacturers want MARKET SHARE. They want people to try their products, enjoy the products, and become repeat customers. Who is most likely to become a repeat buyer of higher-priced items? That's right: affluent households. The food manufacturer would jump for joy if they saw you, an affluent shopper, using their coupon to buy their product. THIS IS WHY THEY PAY TO PRINT THE

# COUPONS IN THE FIRST PLACE!

Grocers make money every time a shopper selects their store over the competition. They want you in their store and they want you to fill your cart with the best items in their store They're not worried about processing a few coupons if it keeps you coming back.

**MYTH 8: It doesn't make sense to buy products that I don't normally buy.**

**REALITY:** Again, let's look at this situation from the food manufacturer's perspective. They develop new lines of products, new flavors, new combinations, etc., because they believe that consumers will like them. No company would incur the massive expense of testing, packaging, and distributing a product if they didn't believe the buying public would like it. They are DESPERATE to have you buy a box of their latest creation and let your family try it. By printing coupons that offer you a large discount on the product, they want to overcome any price resistance and the natural tendency to avoid trying something unfamiliar. So guess what: once you try the product, chances are high that you and/or your family will LOVE IT. And when you go to buy the product again, you won't have a coupon – but you WILL have the request from your family to 'get more' of the product. So the hope is that you will become a loyal purchaser and you will pay full-price for the item – this time, the next time, and on and on for years. This is the manufacturer's goal, and it works: my kids ask me to buy specific brand names of items that they enjoyed the first time I bought them (brands they wouldn't even know about if I hadn't made the initial purchase using a store coupon.) Couponing works for everyone – it works for the manufacturer who sells more products, it works for the store manager who makes his or her money whether you use the coupon or not, and it works for your family: you get cheap or FREE stuff initially, and you get to try the best new and improved products that the industry has to offer.

The people employed by the leading food manufacturers are not stupid; they're actually very smart. They're not putting coupons out there to be charitable. They're attempting to BUY your loyalty...

**MYTH 9: I make a good living. Why would someone like ME need to use grocery coupons?**

**REALITY:** Few people are doing as well as they could be. Just about everyone could benefit from saving money. Examples:

1. Do you currently owe a balance on a credit cards? If you answered YES, you've just lost your vote. If you don't mind paying hundreds of dollars in interest each year, you're right – you don't need to use coupons but you <u>DO</u> need to have your head examined!

2. Do you owe ANY money on ANY loan, including your home mortgage? Couponing could save you $5,000 per year. Imagine what your loan balances would look like if you paid down $5,000 per year. Case closed.

3. Do you have the very latest clothing, cars, electronics, home furnishings, etc.? If not, why don't you run out today and pay cash for everything you've ever wanted? If you could, you're right: you don't need to save money. If you honestly couldn't pay cash on the barrel today, you need to save more money, and couponing is a step in the right direction.

4. Do you honestly have more money than you need? If so, give some to charity, and save some for your own use. You'll feel better about it.

Save your pennies, nickels, dimes and dollars now! Because if you spend like there's no tomorrow – there might not BE a tomorrow. At least not the same tomorrow as today. *(Yogi Berra should have said that…)*

**MYTH 10: Couponing is hard to do, and a real waste of time.**

**REALITY:** If you do it right, couponing will only add one or two hours to your shopping time per week and it can easily save you $50 per week on groceries  Plus, it can be fun. If you are independently wealthy, or simply don't care about money, couponing is not for you. Or, if you have some other method to earn $1,000, $2,000 or more per year in your spare time – without working – and it's something that you enjoy , you should pursue it. Yes, couponing takes a little effort. But the ends justify the means.

If your spare time truly is worth more than $50 per hour, consider hiring a neighborhood kid to clip your coupons for $10 per hour; it's less work for them than clipping your lawn. And for you, it's the chance to make $40 an hour without lifting a finger...or even a pair of scissors...

## Big Idea Recap – Chapter 5

*BIG IDEA 11:* *The richest people in the world still do many things the way they did early in their life, because that is what made them rich.*

*BIG IDEA 12:* *Saving money is the same thing as EARNING money. If you have an easy way to 'turn on the tap' to put more money in your pocket, you're very lucky. If you're like the 99% of us who have to live on a fixed income or a regular paycheck, open your mind to ways that you can SAVE money and do more with what you've got.*

*BIG IDEA 13:* *If you have credit card balances or any amount of consumer debt, you need to GET OUT OF DEBT as quickly as you can. Save money on groceries, and use the money to pay off your debt quicker.*

*BIG IDEA 14:* *Write smaller checks to your grocery store, and you'll have more money left in your checking account at the end of the day. Yes, this is simple math – but sometimes the obvious doesn't hit home until you think about it...*

*BIG IDEA 15:* *All grocery products were new at some point in time. You've been buying your favorites your whole life. Maybe you'll find some new favorites if you just try them one time?*

*BIG IDEA 16:* *Smart money management never goes out of style. But weak money management can seriously cramp your style. Maybe not today – but later in the month or later in the year – and certainly later in life. Pennies that you save today will compound into dollars over time. Conversely, small debt that you start to rack up today will compound into larger debt over time, and that can be very hard to overcome.*

**BIG IDEA 17:** *Don't worry about taking money out of the pockets of the major food manufacturing companies. They don't worry about overcharging you... and they're already rich!*

**BIG IDEA 18:** *Grocers make money every time a shopper selects their store over the competition. They want you in their store, and they want you to fill your cart as high as it will go, with the best items in their store. They're not worried about accepting a few coupons if it keeps you coming back.*

**BIG IDEA 19:** *The people employed by the leading food manufacturers are not stupid; in fact, they're actually very, very smart. They're not putting coupons out there to be charitable; they're issuing them to gain market share and win your loyalty. You might even say – perish the thought – that they're attempting to BUY your loyalty...*

**BIG IDEA 20:** *Later in life, you probably won't make the same income that you make today. Save money NOW while you've still got it – and you'll have a lot more money later in life when you'll need it more.*

**BIG IDEA 21:** *If your time truly is worth more than $50 per hour, consider hiring a neighborhood kid to clip your coupons for $10 per hour; it's less work for him or her than clipping your lawn. And for you, it's like making $40 an hour without lifting a finger. Or a pair of scissors...*

**BIG IDEA 22:** *Be charitable to yourself by using coupons and selecting brands that are on sale. If you really don't need to save money, give it to a real charity; you'll feel better, and so will they.*

# Chapter 6: Strategy and Tactics:
# How To Win the War for Your Wallet

As any military strategist will tell you, there are two parts to any battle plan:

a.      **STRATEGY.** This is the creation of a PLAN. Generals always plan before they implement an attack on the battlefield.

b.      **TACTICS.** This is the actual implementation of the plan.

The secret to tackling any major goal is to PLAN YOUR WORK, then WORK YOUR PLAN. Let's look at the STRATEGY behind couponing, and the many rules, regulations and insider tips you'll need to know before you hit the grocery store.

The battle to save money at the grocery store begins long before you set foot in the store. Think of the actual process of grocery shopping as being like a football game. Players train and exercise for months before they play the first game of the season. They are in excellent physical condition and are well-versed on their team's playbook long before the first ball is hiked. The "grocery game" is a lot like a football game: If you PLAN to save money and are PREPARED to save money before you hit the aisles of your grocery store, you WILL save money.

## BASIC COUPONING STRATEGY

Here are the 10 "sacred rules" of couponing. Learn them. Live them.

**1. EXPIRATION:** Check expiration dates religiously before you shop. NEVER try to use an expired coupon.

**2. DOUBLING:** Find out if the grocery store offers DOUBLE COUPON redemption. If not, leave immediately and find a store that does.

**3. DOUBLING LIMITS:** Find out the maximum coupon value for doubling, i.e. up to 50¢, up to 60¢, up to 99¢, etc. Also find out if the store limits the number of coupons you can redeem in one visit, (e.g. 20 coupon maximum per visit.)

**4. BOGO POLICY:** Find out the store's policy on BOGO (Buy One / Get One Free) specials, (can you buy only 1, or must you buy 2?)

**5. CLIP EVERYTHING.** Clip and keep ALL coupons for products you may want, even low-value coupons. *(HINT: The highest-value coupon may not provide the best overall value.)*

**6. BRAND REQUIREMENTS.** Most coupons are brand specific. NEVER try to redeem a coupon for a brand other than the one shown on the coupon.

**7. QUANTITY REQUIREMENTS:** Does the coupon require you to buy 2 or more of the item to get the discount?

**8. CONTAINER SIZE / FLAVOR REQUIREMENTS:** Is the coupon redeemable for all sizes, flavors and variations of the product, or is there a specific choice requirement defined on the coupon?

**9. MATCHING REQUIREMENTS:** Is a matching purchase needed to redeem the coupon, e.g. buy milk & cookies to get X¢ off on the cookies?

**10. HYPER VALUES.** Look for items that are on sale that you have a coupon for. You will enjoy a double discount that gives you the item for a very low cost, or even FREE in some cases!

Let's review each of these 10 strategy items in detail.

**EXPIRATION**
Food companies issue coupons to boost seasonal sales of their products. Almost every coupon you clip will have an expiration date. The scanners in most grocery stores identify each coupon by linking the barcode on your coupon to a database of valid coupons in circulation. If your coupon is expired, the scanner will catch it instantly. Many check out clerks check the expiration date before they scan the coupon. Plus, if you knowingly attempt to redeem an expired coupon you are committing attempted fraud. Coupons are negotiable documents. They have real value, especially to the grocer who accepts them. Take a minute to scan through ALL of your coupons before

you go shopping so you can stay on the right side of the law... and your store manager. *(It's unlikely that anyone has ever served jail time for attempting to redeem an expired grocery coupon. But just bear in mind that the store is simply the brokering agent for the coupon. If they accept a coupon that is expired, they have no chance of getting credit for it. So you are really attempting to steal from the store. Do it once too often, and your store manager may choose to call you out on it...)*

The expiration date can actually work in your favor, so there's another reason to be aware of coupons that are almost at their expiration date (but not beyond it.) As I stated above, the food companies use coupons to boost seasonal sales of their products. So when they issue a coupon on January 1st with an expiration date of March 31st, they are anticipating a 'bell curve' in their response. It looks something like this:

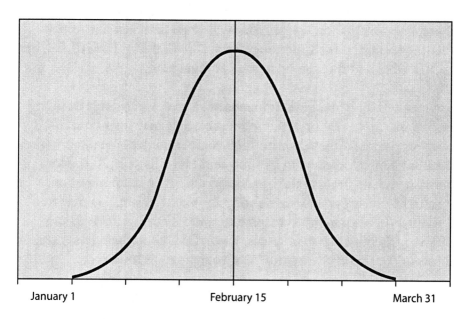

| January 1 | February 15 | March 31 |

The day the coupons are distributed, they start to appear in stores. Over the next few weeks, more and more consumers redeem the coupons, so the total number of coupons redeemed goes up. At some point near the middle of the promotion, the volume of coupons redeemed hits a peak. From that point on, the total number starts to decline and eventually trails off.

If you charted out the total number of coupons redeemed from January 1st through March 31st, you would see that very few coupons are redeemed in the last week of the promotion – between March 24th & March 31st. If you were a product manager at the food company, you would be concerned about declining sales at this point, and may do something to boost sales until the next coupons are distributed. This is when many products are put on special, or offered as a 'BOGO'. See the 'BOGO' section later in this book to find out how this works.

## DOUBLING

Coupon doubling is a popular technique used by grocery stores to attract shoppers, especially senior citizens and families with children. It's almost mandatory when there are multiple grocers in your area competing for your business. The retailers know that only a small percentage of shoppers will actually take advantage of this offer – and those shoppers that do use coupons will often have just one or two that they found in their morning paper. VERY FEW PEOPLE USE COUPONS and this can be to your advantage.

In areas with only marginal competition, a grocer may limit doubling to coupons up to 30¢ or 35¢ in value, and they may set a limit of 10 coupons per visit. In areas with high competition, it's common to see doubling limits increased to 99¢ in value, and a limit of 20 coupons per visit – or no limit at all. In areas of EXTREME competition where the grocery chains are fighting for market share, you may find TRIPLING of coupons from time to time. When you see a store offering tripling of coupon values, you MUST shop there to get the most for your money – regardless of your store preference.

**Some important rules to know about doubling:**

1. Find out if your store doubles "DO NOT DOUBLE" coupons. Some manufacturers are printing the words "DO NOT DOUBLE" in the margins of the coupon. Your store may or may not choose to double the coupon – and unless you know their policy for certain, avoid these coupons if you are not willing to settle for the face discount value.

2. Determine the net redemption value of your coupon before you get to the checkout counter. You may want to use a lower-value coupon, which could net out a greater discount for you. More about this later.

It's true. Check the prices for ALL brands for which you have coupons. You can eventually achieve a lower net-cost per unit by selecting a brand for which you have a lower-value coupon, IF the store has the item on sale. Here is an example:

| Brand Name | Store Price | Coupon Value | Net Cost To You After Coupon Doubling |
|---|---|---|---|
| Brand A Spaghetti Sauce | $2.59 | $1.00 | $1.59 *(coupon not doubled)* |
| Brand B Spaghetti Sauce | $2.29 on sale | $.55 | $1.19 |

As you can see, you will save 40¢ by choosing Brand B – EVEN THOUGH your coupon had about half the face value of the coupon for Brand A. Two factors have contributed to your savings here:

**a. Store sale.** The price savings on Brand B seems very small but can often make a huge net difference in your total grocery bill.

**b. Doubling value of the coupon.** A lesser-value coupon that is doubled can be worth more than a larger coupon that is NOT doubled. Again, the coupon net value difference here seems negligible – only 10¢ net difference. But combined with the sale price, the net savings effect is multiplied.

## DOUBLING LIMITS

Every grocery store sets its own limits on the high value of coupon doubling. The most common level you will find is 50¢, although some stores go as low as 35¢ and some go as high as 99¢. You must know the doubling limit of the store you are shopping in, BEFORE you shop there. If you don't, you will very likely be disappointed at the check out counter.

When you view the face value of your store coupons, you should get in the habit of determining their actual redemption value in the store you are shopping in. This will take a little practice, but it will pay off big time in terms of savings. Here are some examples on how you should train your mind to think of coupons of different valuations. This example is for a store that has set a 55¢ maximum value on coupon doubling.

| Coupon Face Value | Redemption Value After Doubling |
|---|---|
| 25¢ | 50¢ |
| 35¢ | 70¢ |
| 55¢ | $1.10 |
| 60¢ | 60¢ |
| 75¢ | 75¢ |

As you can see, the highest value coupon does NOT always result in the greatest discount. This is why knowing the doubling limit of your grocery store is so important.

Sometimes, the lower the coupon value, the greater the net discount. Smaller-value coupons can often lead to larger savings at the grocery store.

## BOGO POLICY

Remember those old 'alien from outer space' movies where the jet pilot reported a "Bogie at 10:00?" You need to be on similar high alert in the grocery store: "BOGO in aisle 10!" What is a BOGO? It's a "Buy One / Get One" deal; you get the second item for FREE when you buy one at the regular price.

Why do stores offer BOGOs?

**1. OVERSTOCK.** They may have ordered too many of a given item and they simply do not have room to store them. Alternatively, the cost of storing the excess items may be excessive. It may be cheaper to clear the item out at half the price.

**2. EXPIRATION DATE.** Perhaps the items did not sell as quickly as the store manager had anticipated and the inventory is approaching its expiration date. The items must sell before the expiration date or be discarded at a 100% loss to the store when the expiration date is reached.

**3. MANUFACTURER PROMOTION.** To build market share for a specific product in a specific store, the manufacturer's representative may give the store free merchandise to give away under a BOGO deal.

**4. LOSS LEADER.** The store may be in an intense market share fight with a competitor. By advertising a number of BOGO deals, they can often entice shoppers to change their store of preference. Shoppers may visit one time to get the BOGO deals, and the manager is hoping they enjoy the shopping experience and the values enough to switch stores permanently.

Grocery stores will blast their BOGO deals in big type on the front page of their flyers. They will NOT advertise their actual BOGO redemption policy. Why? Because they have nothing to gain by doing so. Many shoppers will assume that if an item is on BOGO special, they can buy just one and pay half the price. This is not always the case, and in many stores it is NEVER the case. You cannot be timid when it comes to knowing the store's policy on BOGOs. Be bold: walk up to the customer service counter and ask the manager whether you MUST buy 2 of the item, or whether you can buy just one at half the price. It is your right to know, and it can make a big difference in your checkout total.

If you honestly don't need two of an item, or you cannot use two containers before the expiration date, it makes no sense to buy the extra (second) item. However, if the BOGO is for a non-perishable item that you could use in the future, buy two and put the extra item in your pantry or freezer. You could also consider donating it to Second Harvest or your local food bank. If you were going to buy the item anyway, do not pass up the BOGO deal; someone can use the second item, and they'll be glad to get it.

BOGO promotions are quick for a retailer to implement. Many times they are store-specific, (although they are often chain-wide promotions offered by the leading grocers.) A store may offer a quick two or three day BOGO promotion to clear out stockpiled inventory. This is the ideal time to use your store coupon. Here's an example to help you understand why:

| PRODUCT: | Gummy Gunk Cereal, 21 oz. Box, regular price $3.50. |
|---|---|
| COUPON VALUE: | 50¢ off on one box purchase. Store doubles the coupon value to $1.00. |
| BOGO SALE PRICE: | Buy one at $3.50, get one free. |
| NET COST TO YOU: | $2.50 for two boxes of cereal, $1.25 each. |

You have now saved $2.25 per box of cereal, for a grand total savings of $4.50 – more than 54% OFF RETAIL!

SUPER SECRET: Some stores have altered their BOGO policy to meet the needs of senior citizens. Seniors who live alone often do not need two boxes of a product; they consume so little that the second box would become stale before they use it. To keep senior customers happy, many stores will allow you to buy one box at half price, rather than buy one at full price and take a second box free. CHECK WITH YOUR STORE BEFORE YOU BUY! If your store allows half off purchasing of one item in a BOGO deal, look how much you could save in this same example:

| PRODUCT: | Gummy Gunk Cereal, 21 oz. Box, regular price $3.50. |
|---|---|
| COUPON VALUE: | 50¢ off on one box purchase. Store doubles the coupon value to $1.00. |
| BOGO SALE PRICE AT STORE WITH "1/2 OFF ONE" POLICY: | Buy one at $1.75. |
| NET COST TO YOU: | $0.75 for one box of cereal. |

You have now saved $2.75 off normal retail on one box of cereal, a savings of over 73% OFF RETAIL!

## CLIP EVERYTHING

Let's cut to the chase: there is no need to clip coupons for 'Super Sugar Shack' cereal if you're a senior and don't have grandkids. And there is no need to clip a coupon for denture cream if you're twenty-five and have a full set of pearly whites. What I mean by 'Clip Everything' is do not avoid coupons for brands you haven't tried, or coupons that at first glance seem worthless. You might like the brands you haven't tried, and you'll especially like them if you get them for FREE or close to free. And the 'nickel and dime' coupons that you might think worthless can really add up in certain situations. Here's an example:

| Item | Original Price | Sale Price | Coupon Value | Doubled Value | Net Cost To You | % Savings Off Original Price |
|------|---------|-------|--------|---------|---------|---------------|
| Ketchup | $1.29 | 99¢ | 25¢ | 50¢ | 49¢ | 63% |
| Hot Sauce | 79¢ | 59¢ | 30¢ | 60¢ | FREE | 100% |
| Crackers | $1.69 | $1.29 | 50¢ | $1.00 | 29¢ | 82% |

Many people will pass over a 30¢ coupon as trivial, and not clip it. But as you can see in our example, it can lead to getting a product totally FREE. And that's just about the best possible way to stretch your grocery budget. Plus, it results in what you will come to know as 'Coupon Nirvana', a feeling of euphoria and power. It's not the free merchandise that is the reward; it's the thrill of the hunt. If you follow my techniques for regular, systematic couponing, it is a thrill you will enjoy every week, over and over again.

## BRAND REQUIREMENTS

When a coupon says it is good for Brand A Peanut Butter, it means that it is ONLY good for Brand A Peanut Butter, not Brand B or Brand C. After all, the Brand A marketing people spent big bucks to get that coupon into distribution, and they deserve the sale it generates. No legitimate grocer would accept a coupon for a brand other than the one shown.

Where this gets tricky is when the coupon is for a 'family' of products. For example, some cereal companies will issue coupons good for two or more boxes of any brand of cereal they make. A good way to tell is to look at the photo on the coupon, which will typically show each brand they manufacture. OR, you can look at the logos on the box to verify that it's one of their brands. Be doubly careful about checking that you receive your discount on these types of coupons, because they often won't scan properly.

Another thing to watch is that you select the BRAND VARIATION a given coupon is valid for. The industry calls these "line extensions", and they may have five or even ten line extensions in the same food category. They're great for finicky eaters, but bad if you select the wrong variation and have to pay full price for it. This is especially true with brands that have extensive product lines such as 'healthy' or 'diet' foods. You may see the brand name on the package and think it is the product described on the coupon, only to realize at the checkout line that the coupon is for a different implementation of the same brand. For example, one frozen dinner manufacturer offers "Duos", "Singles", "Grilled Specialties" and "Bowls". All four are frozen dinners, but the coupon may be valid for only one of these four types of frozen dinners. The scanner will reject the coupon if you haven't selected the exact same type shown on the coupon. If you see a wall full of products with the same brand logo, be on the alert that it's easy to select the wrong product. You should always double-check the flavor or brand variation.

**SIGNS LIE.** Another thing I'd like to point out about Brand Requirements is that you can't believe your eyes when it comes to signs, sign placement, and sign wording. I had an experience recently where the store's print ad said that a particular brand of bacon was on BOGO sale. There was a giant display sign in the middle of three different variations of the brand's bacon. The immediate inclination is to assume that all three of these variations were on sale, so just go ahead and pick any two and get the deal. WRONGO-PONGO! The ad stated that the "Natural Choice" version was on sale, but the sign was placed among the regular versions of the product. The variation that was on sale wasn't even near the display sign! Was this an intentional deception on the part of the store manager, or simply an honest mistake on the part of a sleepy stock clerk? You be the judge... but the price of the sale bacon was $4.99 for two (net cost $2.50 per package), and the price of the NON-sale bacon was $5.99 per individual package. If you picked up two of the non-sale variation, you'd pay about $7.00 extra for the same amount of meat. Bringing home the bacon gets a lot more expensive if you aren't on the alert.

And given that the sale sign was in the largest portion of the meat cooler among the largest inventory of all the brands of bacon sold in that store, I would tend to think that a lot of shoppers made a mistake in their selection. And once you've left the store, there is nothing you can do about it; you can't return food if there was no mistake on the store's part. All you can do is to be more careful in the future. So don't believe what you see; believe what you verify before you check out.

**FLYERS LIE.** If you find a sales flyer in your shopping cart, don't use it until you verify that it's the current flyer. The clerks don't necessarily clean out the shopping carts every day. So a flyer you find in the cart on a Sunday could have expired the day before. Check the dates first.

**SALES CLERKS LIE.** When an item rings up wrong, I've had sales clerks state with 100% certainty, "that item was on sale last week, but it's not on sale now." I pull out the current sales flyer and show them the item. All of a sudden, they're not so certain, and in fact they seem ticked that they were caught in a lie. So don't be afraid to stick to your guns, especially when you know you're right.

## QUANTITY REQUIREMENTS

Some coupons require multiple purchases, i.e. "Save $1.00 on 2". These type of coupons should put up red flags in your mind:
a. Do I need two of this item, and will I consume this quantity within the normal shelf life of the product?
b. The face value of the coupon is automatically cut in HALF, because you must buy two of them. Factor this in when you are doing your 'net cost' calculations.

The one time that this quantity issue goes away is when the item is on BOGO (Buy One / Get One FREE). The cashier will scan two boxes of the product, so you will have technically purchased two, and the coupon will be authorized. But you will only be charged for one item, and you will still enjoy the full value of the coupon discount.

# CONTAINER SIZE / FLAVOR REQUIREMENTS

This is another area where discretion is the better part of valor. You have to understand that there are over 10,000 items in the typical grocery store. The manufacturer may have an interest in promoting sales of their 32 oz. bottle, and is trying to sway people away from buying the 16 oz. bottle. So if the coupon says the discount is valid on the 32 oz. bottle only, that is the rule. The scanner will not accept the coupon if you try to use it with a 16 oz. bottle.

The same rule applies to flavors. The coupon may say that the discount is available on the "barbeque" flavor of sauce. You may find that there are three other flavor choices on the shelf. There is no hard-and-fast rule about this, because sometimes the coupon is valid for all four flavors, and in other cases it is valid for the one flavor only. If in doubt, take the coupon and the flavor you want to the Customer Service window and ask. They will scan the product and the coupon and let you know if the coupon is valid on that specific variation of the product.

# MATCHING REQUIREMENTS

If a coupon offer looks too good to be true, be sure to read the fine print. It may require a matching purchase. For example, the coupon may say "FREE half-gallon of milk". The fine type may include the actual offer: Free milk when you buy a 16 oz. package of our cookies AND an 18 oz. box of our cereal. Bear in mind that they are counting on you to pay the full retail price of their cookies ($3.50) and the full retail price of their cereal ($4.35). So you must spend $7.85 to get a 'free' half-gallon of milk ($2.00). You may actually come out ahead buying store brand cookies and cereal, and paying the regular price for your milk. It pays to do the math quickly in your head before using a matching requirement coupon.

One way to get increased value through 'matching requirement coupons' is to use ANOTHER coupon for the items required. In other words, in the example above, you may find that you have a different coupon for the required brand of cookies, and possibly a third coupon for the particular brand of cereal. In most cases, the store's computer will not consider these to be competing coupons. So if you had a 50¢ coupon for the cookies and a 35¢ coupon for the cereal, you could get $1.70 in doubled value for these coupons, plus the cashier will take off the $1.50 for the milk. You never know until you try. In most cases, the cashier must manually enter the price of the free item into the cash register, so the coupon is entered differently from the others and the store's computer will not reject it as an attempted double redemption.

## HYPER VALUES

If you use only one strategy out of these coupon value-increasing ideas, make sure you understand and use the strategy of 'Hyper Values'. Here's how it works:

Let's say that your store is overstocked with a certain brand and size of canned peaches; they offer them at 50% off. Instead of 99¢, they're marked down to 50¢. You happen to have a coupon for this brand offering 25¢ off a single can of fruit. Since the store will automatically double the coupon at check-out time, you are now getting the peaches for FREE. It just doesn't get any better than this.

**BONUS BUYS.** Another example is the 'Bonus Buys' that a store will offer. If they are overstocked on a particular manufacturer's line of cereal – or perhaps the manufacturer's rep really needs to boost volume in your area and extends special pricing to the store – you may find that your store extends a 'Bonus Buy' across the entire product line. A typical example of this is in cereals: All Brand "A" cereals on a list will be 3 for $5.00. (Be sure to check the product name and package size requirements; the bonus may apply to the 28 oz. box of cereal and NOT the 18 oz. box of cereal – so you could end up paying MORE for a SMALLER box if you're not careful!) If you have a coupon for $1.00 off on any 3 boxes of Brand "A" cereal, use it. You'll now be paying $4.00 for 3 boxes of cereal, or approximately $1.33 per box.

**IF THERE'S NO SIGN, IT MUST BE ON SALE.** It's important to note that many of the special deals available at a store are NOT advertised on the store shelf. The only way you'll find them is to read the flyer that shows up in your morning newspaper, typically on a

Wednesday or Thursday. These same flyers are also available on a rack when you enter the store. What is really laughable is that literally NOBODY picks up a flyer when they enter the store. How many times have you seen somebody poring over a store flyer before they shop? Almost never. The reason? It's déclassé, and most people 'just don't have time for that'. Again, if your time is more valuable than your money, breeze on by the stack of flyers. The 2 minutes you save by NOT reading the flyer could end up costing you $10, $20 or more. (But hey, it's only money).

## Big Idea Recap – Chapter 6

*BIG IDEA 23: The greatest savings in the "grocery game" are achieved when you PLAN in advance to save money and are PREPARED to save money before you ever hit the aisles of your grocery store.*

*BIG IDEA 24: The closer to the coupon expiration date, the greater the chances that an additional promotion on the product has already started. It means that you can save even more on the same product.*

*BIG IDEA 25: The food manufacturers know that many people will NEVER clip a coupon. For every person who REDEEMS a coupon, 10 others will READ the coupons and associate those brands with value. In other words, coupons are used to build impressions in your mind that certain products offer excellent quality AND value – regardless of whether they actually do or not. Unless you actually clip and redeem the coupon, you won't receive that extra value.*

*BIG IDEA 26: Watch for 'tripling' events. This is when a store offers triple the face value of the coupon. Some stores limit this promotion to 50¢, but others will triple up to 99¢ – so many of your items will be totally free after the discount.*

*BIG IDEA 27: Sometimes, the lower the coupon value, the greater the net discount. (WHAT? Did I read that right, or is it a typographical error?) No, you did not read it incorrectly. Smaller-value coupons can often lead to larger savings at the grocery store.*

**BIG IDEA 28:** *Take advantage of BOGO deals on non-perishable items, even when you don't have an immediate need for the item. Canned goods or cleaning supplies will keep just fine for a year or two on the shelf – and you won't have to pay full-price the next time you need the item.*

**BIG IDEA 29:** *If your grocer allows you to buy only one item at half-price under a 'BOGO' deal AND you are using a coupon on the purchase, your net savings amount for the one item will be much higher that if you purchased two units of the same item.*

**BIG IDEA 30:** *Clip every coupon that is for a product that some member of your household could use, even if you've never tried the brand before. You might find a super-special on the item, and you might end up liking it more than your current brand.*

**BIG IDEA 31:** *Check, double-check, even triple-check to make sure that the brand variation shown on your coupon is the same as the item you put into your shopping cart. If it's wrong, you will probably end up paying full price for the item.*

**BIG IDEA 32:** *Don't make assumptions when selecting items that are on sale. Pick up a sales flyer when you first enter the store, and compare the wording & photo of the sale item to the item in your shopping cart; if it doesn't match exactly, investigate until you are certain that you have the correct sale item. Don't trust signs or sales flyers until you verify that the dates and brand variations shown are correct.*

**BIG IDEA 33:** *Be wary of "save on 2" or "save on 3" coupons. You have to buy so many of the item, it can negate the net value of the coupon.*

**BIG IDEA 34:** *If a coupon shows a photo of a particular flavor, don't assume it's valid for all flavors unless this is specifically stated on the coupon.*

**BIG IDEA 35:** *If the purchase of 2 or 3 different items is required to get a free item, you may be able to use additional coupons to lower the cost of the 2 or 3 items individually.*

**BIG IDEA 36:** *You can get certain items for FREE is you have a coupon* for sale items and your store doubles the value of your coupon. Read the ads, match your coupons to the ads, and do the math. It's that easy.

**BIG IDEA 37:** Sometimes buying the bigger box costs less than buying the smaller box.

**BIG IDEA 38:** The store is <u>not</u> required to call your attention to the items that are on sale. To get the best values you have to take note of the items that are featured in the store's sales flyer, find those items, verify that you have selected the EXACT size / brand / variation that is on sale, and purchase those items. The sale items won't jump into your cart by themselves (but if you're not careful, similar products that you THINK are on sale but are actually NOT on sale, will be the ones that end up in your cart...)

# Chapter 7: Couponing Tactics: The Simplest Way to Organize Coupons

There are many different gadgets and custom wallets on the market to help you organize your coupons. Some cost only a few dollars, others cost $15, $20 or more. YOU DON'T NEED THEM! There's a method I use that is basically free, uncomplicated, and flexible. It's simple, it's easy to remember, and once you get the hang of it, it will make finding your coupons a breeze.

Use 8 ordinary white envelopes. If you're super-cheap, you can even re-use bank envelopes, payroll envelopes, or business reply envelopes from your junk mail, *(now that's REALLY cheap.)* When the envelopes wear out, simply replace them. I keep mine bundled with a rubber band, and I store them in the glove box of my car. That way, I always know where they are. Also, they're easy to stick in a pocket when I head into the store.

The 8 envelopes are categories of products and stores. Write the category and item listings on each of your envelopes, as follows:

## BAKED GOODS
- Bread / Baking Supplies
- Refrigerated Dinner Rolls / Biscuits
- Cereal
- Cookies / Crackers
- Chips / Candy / Nuts / Popcorn / Snacks

## CANNED GOODS & BEVERAGES
- Vegetables
- Salad
- Soup
- Fruit
- Juices / Soda
- Coffee

## MEAT & FROZEN
- Lunchmeats

- Bacon / Sausage / Fresh Meats
- Any Frozen Product (except Ice Cream)

## CONDIMENTS & SIDE DISHES
- Pasta / Sauces
- Boxed Meal Mixes
- Rice / Grains
- Salad Dressing
- Peanut Butter / Jelly
- Spices / Salt / Sugar
- Cooking Oil

## DAIRY
- Milk / Cheese / Sour Cream
- Eggs
- Ice Cream / Toppings
- Pudding / Dips

## CLEANING SUPPLIES
- Household Cleaning Products
- Paper Products
- Dog / Cat Food

## PERSONAL PRODUCTS
- Personal Hygiene Items / Soaps / Deodorant
- Medicine

## RESTAURANT & STORE DISCOUNTS
- Store Discount Coupons (i.e. $5.00 off any $30 Order)
- Restaurant / Retail Store Coupons
- Specific-Store Coupons, i.e. Drug Store Coupons

## HOW TO ORGANIZE YOUR COUPONS

First off, it's important that you dedicate yourself to saving money. If you can't set aside 15 minutes per week to deal with your coupons, the system won't work. You should simply spend the extra $30, $40, $50 or more and use your 15 minutes for more productive things – like watching TV, reading a magazine or talking on the phone. Yes, I'm being sarcastic, but the truth of the matter is that saving money takes time and dedication. You have to have an almost religious zeal for following the system (or whatever system you prefer) and stick to it.

It's like anything else – a diet, a hobby, or a sport – you have to do the same things like clockwork for an extended period of time before you will ever see any results.

I find that it helps to set a specific time, place and routine for organizing and maintaining your coupons, as follows:

– **CENTRAL LOCATION.** Keep all coupons in one place until they are sorted. I use a small wicker basket, and simply put the Sunday coupon sections in there until I have time to go through them.

– **CLIP ALL AT ONCE.** When you have the time, go through the coupon sections and cut out any coupon you might consider using. It's important that you do not reject coupons by brand name or familiarity at this point. If it's something you wouldn't even consider using, obviously don't clip that coupon. But if it's something that you'd consider trying if it was free, clip the coupon: it may end up free to you if you play your coupons right...

– **REVIEW EXPIRATION DATES.** Before going on a shopping trip (or at least once every few weeks), go through your envelopes and remove all expired coupons. NEVER try to use an out-of-date coupon. It's bad form, it can be embarrassing, and, if you do it knowingly, it can actually be illegal.

– **SORT ALL AT ONCE.** I keep my coupon envelopes held together with a rubber band. When it's time to do my sorting, I open the envelopes one by one and pull out any expired coupons. Then, I lay the envelopes out on the table in 2 rows, in a specific order:

• Left row top to bottom: Meats, Canned Goods, Side Dishes
• Right row top to bottom: Breads, Dairy, Cleaning Supplies
• I put the final two envelopes to the side, because you really don't tend to get as many coupons in the Personal Products and Restaurant

& Store Discount categories. Most of your coupons will be in the "big six", so I tend to focus on those most of all; it's just mentally easier.

The benefit of following a routine is that you end up sorting without having to think about it, i.e. lunch meat / frozen foods always go to the top left, bread & cereal is always top right, etc. I leave plenty of room between the envelopes, and simply stack my new coupons immediately below each of the envelopes. Then, when I'm done, I put the new coupons in the envelopes, bundle the envelopes back up with my rubber band, and throw away my pile of expired coupons.

Of course, you can develop your own routine. The most important thing is that you establish a fixed routine. Do it the same way each week, follow each step to its completion in a quick and determined manner, and do it all at once. This will make short work out of organizing your coupons, and will make it more relaxing and stress-free. Remember, anything you can do to save time with your system will make it easier to follow, and easier to stick to.

If you make a ROUTINE out of PLANNING to save money, sticking to your PLAN will help you ROUTINELY save money.


**SHOPPING TIME: organize your shopping trip to save time and keep food fresh.**

Health experts will tell you to shop the perimeter of a grocery store first. If you do this, you'll load up on fresh fruits & vegetables, baked goods, meats, etc., and avoid the processed foods on the inner aisles. It's a good thought, but not always practical if you've got a family and have to stock up on a wide range of items every time you shop. If you follow the expert's advice, you'll have a lot of perishable items in your cart that will melt or lose freshness while you are browsing the inner aisles of the grocery store.

For example, if you buy fresh meats and you put them in your cart first, they could be out of refrigeration for 45, 60, even 90 minutes. Add in your drive time home, and you could be keeping them out of refrigeration for a dangerous amount of time. Of course, this doesn't apply to produce, and that's the place to start shopping first. There is literally nothing you can buy in the store that is better for your family's health than fresh fruit and vegetables. It takes a little discipline, but your family will eat healthier if you focus your shopping in this section. Save the bread, dairy products, meat and frozen foods for last, and they'll arrive home in much better condition.

## THE SYSTEM

There are four simple steps when using store coupons:
**1. SCAN** all products in the category to see what's on sale today.
**2. REVIEW** all coupons that you have for the category to see if you have coupons for the items that are on sale.
**3. MATCH.** When you have a match of coupon and sale item put the item in your cart.
**4. POCKET**. Immediately put the coupon in your designated coupon pocket or other storage place.

Let's review why each of these steps is critical to your couponing success.

**SCAN.** When you have an appealing coupon, i.e. $1.00 off on an item we'll call 'Brand A', you may be tempted to search out that exact item and buy it. And chances are, you'll get a good value by buying Brand A. But you may not be enjoying the BEST value. Let's say that Brand A's normal price is $3.99. With your dollar off, you'll pay $2.99. But 'Brand B' may be on sale for $2.49, so when you buy this brand you'll pay less without using a coupon, making Brand B a better value choice right from the start.

As an even better value proposition, consider that you may have a coupon for the Brand B item. Let's say the Brand B coupon is for 50¢ off. Many people would simply look at the two coupons side by side: Brand A's coupon gives you $1.00 off, and Brand B's coupon gives you 50¢ off, so the Brand A coupon offers you better savings, right? WRONG! In this case, the 50¢ Brand B coupon will be doubled in value at the checkout counter, so it's EQUAL in value to Brand A's $1.00 off coupon. Plus, because Brand B is on sale for $2.49, your net cost of buying it will be $1.49 – fully ONE HALF THE NET COST OF THE BRAND A ITEM!!! Over time, you will find that

SCANNING the entire product category before making a selection will be your #1 key to saving.

**REVIEW.** You'll find that in most stores, the higher-priced items will be at eye level. Manufacturers pay a 'slot fee' to buy shelf space, and the highest-price space is right at eye level. Most people are reactive shoppers. They grab the first thing they see that looks appealing. You may notice that the higher-priced brands look better, because these manufacturers put a lot of effort into their packaging. A can of top-priced peas will look delicious and inviting, while a generic can of peas will look lackluster. But when they're cooked and on your table, do you really think your family will not eat the generic peas? Unless they see the cans, they typically won't know the difference.

Yes, I know, not all generics offer the same quality as the top-shelf brands. And frankly, I prefer the 'baby' peas, which go for about three times the cost of generic. But here's a little secret (one I know from having worked at a pickle factory during summer break at college). The plant I worked at manufactured one of the top-selling brands of pickles in the world. What did we do when we reached our quota of the name brand product for the week? Well... we switched out the paper on the labeling machine, and used the generic-brand labels. Yes, folks – it's a little-told secret of the food processing industry. They gear up to keep their factories running 24/7, because that is the only way they can get maximum efficiency and return on investment on their plants. So when their factory reaches their quota of producing the name-brand product, they don't shut down the production line. They change the labels!

If you doubt this, try and run a taste-test contest with your family. Buy two cans of an identical item, one of the high-priced brand and one of the low-priced store brand. Cook both items, and serve them up in identical dishes. See if your family can correctly identify which is the high-priced brand and which is the value brand. I can assure you, the results will be laughable: the value brand will be preferred in many cases.

Another quick test is to compare the bottle design. At my local dollar store, they have a great food products section. They carry lots of condiments and sauces. Their off-brand version of Worcestershire sauce is in a bottle that is shaped remarkably like the #1 brand in the world. When you taste the sauce, it tastes just like the leading brand. I'm not saying that every item you pick up in a dollar store is going to be identical to the leading brand. In fact, some of them will be downright awful. But if you try them, you might find that they're the identical product made by the leading name-brand manufacturer, and you'll enjoy a real deal.

Most of the biggest, most efficient food manufacturing plants produce and package the off-brand products. It may not always be the same quality as the leading brands, but in some cases it is; it would simply be too costly for them to change recipes or ingredients to produce the 'off brands'. So if you're astute and willing to do a little testing, you may get the EXACT SAME QUALITY with a generic or store-brand product.

**MATCH.** You've seen above why it's important to SCAN all of the shelves for the best item and REVIEW all of your coupon and sale combination. Now that you've chosen the best possible combination, you need to MATCH your coupon to the item before you commit to the buy. By this, I mean that you should give a final check of the coupon details and the product details BEFORE you put the item into your cart. Check the brand name, size, flavor, etc., as well as the expiration date. Some brands have four or five categories that are completely different, and the coupon may only be good for one category of item.

Take soup, for example. One top brand sells regular soup, kitchen select soup, chunky soup, home-style soup, and single-serving microwavable soup for one. The coupons they issue are typically good for just one of their soup categories. If you forget to MATCH the specifics of the coupon offer to the EXACT LABEL on the soup can, you could find that your coupon is rejected at the checkout counter – the ultimate coupon-cutter's nightmare.

**POCKET.** Last but not the least, POCKET the coupon. This may seem like a really dumb step, but it's actually very important. You have to physically present ALL of your coupons at the checkout counter when you are buying your groceries. If they don't make it into the hands of the checkout clerk, they won't be redeemed. So it's important to get in the habit of POCKETING all of the coupons you plan to use, and putting them all in one safe secure place. I use my left pocket, but that's just a personal preference. During the course of my shopping trip, if I find that I have an expired coupon, I crush it up and put it in my right pocket, to be thrown away at the first trash can I encounter. Again, that's just the way I do it – and it may not be the best choice for you.

Again, does this sound too elementary and ridiculous to you? It won't, especially if you have ever gotten in your car and realized that you forgot to present your coupons at the checkout counter. You can't go back! Once your shopping transaction is completed, the store won't let you go back and turn your coupons in. So the coupons in your pocket that would have been worth $20 or $30 in actual cash savings will now be worth diddly-squat. You could have taken the family to the movies with that money, but now it's gone.

Here's another reason why you have to be diligent in PHYSICALLY TRANSFERRING THE COUPON to your "POCKET" location for redemption. Have you ever gotten home with your shopping bags and realized that there was an on-pack coupon that you forgot to use? Nothing is more galling than seeing a 50¢ "REDEEM ME NOW" coupon stuck to a box that you have already bought.

Create your own system or use mine. Just make sure you have a true system, and follow it like clockwork. If you do things the same way each week, on every shopping trip, you will systematically save money. And it WILL add up over time.

## Big Idea Recap – Chapter 7

***BIG IDEA 39:*** *The simpler the system, the easier it is to use – and the easier it is to use, the more likely you are to stick with it over time.*

***BIG IDEA 40:*** *If you can't FIND the coupons you need, you can't REDEEM them. Every minute you put into organizing your coupons will* be paid back to you in greater savings at the cash register.

**BIG IDEA 41:** Consistency is the key to effectiveness in any system. Do things the same way every time, and you'll get better at them day after day...

**BIG IDEA 42:** Keep an open mind as to which products you would consider trying. If you only consider buying familiar products or ones you've tried and used before, you'll never maximize your full potential of reducing your food budget. In other words, buying more EXPENSIVE foods could actually SAVE you money.

**BIG IDEA 43:** if you make a ROUTINE out of PLANNING to save money, sticking to your PLAN will help you ROUTINELY save money.

**BIG IDEA 44:** Learn the layout of your grocery store(s). Plan out a mental "road map" of how you will routinely shop in that store. Follow that road map every time you do your big weekly shopping run; you'll become more alert to spotting bargains and avoiding impulse buys, and you'll reduce your in-store time significantly.

**BIG IDEA 45:** Don't let the high price of an item scare you off buying it; similarly, don't let the 'bargain' price of an item make it your #1 choice; calculate the FINAL COST of the item in your head after factoring in the doubled coupon value, and you can actually SAVE MONEY by buying the EXPENSIVE brand!

**BIG IDEA 46:** Most of the biggest, most efficient food manufacturing plants produce and package the off-brand products. If you are astute and willing to do a little testing, you may get the EXACT SAME QUALITY with a generic or store-brand product.

**BIG IDEA 47:** Don't assume that a coupon is good for all sizes / flavors / variations of a particular brand item — even if it seems to be an obvious match. Reading the fine print can save you a bundle at the checkout counter.

**BIG IDEA 48:** Make it a routine to keep your coupons in the EXACT SAME PLACE every time you go shopping; it's a sure way to remember to present them to the cashier before you pay. Remember, once you leave the store, your coupons aren't worth the paper they're printed on...

# Chapter 8: The Currency vs. Coupon Litmus Test

If you are still questioning whether or not you are a "coupon person" (or could ever become one,) here is one sure way to settle the issue once and for all. You may think you're not a candidate to save money, either because you just can't be bothered to clip coupons, or you simply find the whole process distasteful. It's true: some people have complete and total disdain for grocery coupons, and think they aren't worth the paper they're printed on. If you are concerned that you may just be this type of person, try taking the 'Currency vs. Coupon Litmus Test'.

**Step 1.** Locate a paper shredder; chances are there is one somewhere in your office.

**Step 2.** Look in your Sunday newspaper coupon section, and find a 50¢ coupon for a product that your family uses on a regular basis.

**Step 3.** Turn the shredder on, and insert the 50¢ coupon into the shredder. (Feels good, doesn't it?)

**Step 4.** Take a dollar bill out of your wallet or purse.

**Step 5.** Now, insert the dollar bill into the shredder.* *(Hey wait, that's REAL money we're talking about. I don't waste REAL money...!)*

Does shredding the dollar bill bother you more than shredding the coupon? Why? At most grocery stores, the 50¢ coupon would have been doubled in value at the time of redemption, so it is IDENTICAL IN VALUE to the dollar bill. The only difference is that they were issued by different entities: one by the U.S. Mint, and one by a food manufacturer. Keep this one fact in mind: the grocery store cash register doesn't care which is which: it sees both items as having a $1.00 value against the total purchase price of your groceries.

*NOTE: Destruction of U.S. currency is illegal. Do not actually implement this test; it is presented here for comparison purposes only. Okay, and for shock value, too. Wake up and smell the mocha java, people!*

## CLEANLINESS IS NEXT TO GODLINESS: purging your expired coupons.

The couponer's nightmare is thinking you've just scored the ultimate trifecta: BOGO deal, coupon in hand, store sells single item for half the price. Then, the cashier informs you that the coupon you have presented is expired. When you think you're getting a $3.00 item for 29¢ and you have to pay $1.59 for it, you're still getting a great deal – but it's a huge let-down because you got tripped up by the fundamentals. I sometimes get in a hurry, and to be perfectly honest with you, I only purge my coupons about once every month or so. It only takes an extra 15 minutes or so when you're adding new coupons, but sometimes you just don't have those extra 15 minutes. If this is your situation, just take an extra second to check the expiration date before you transfer the coupon to your left pocket. I've caught myself about to make a mistake like this many times.

Some people say, "don't you feel like you've wasted a lot of time when you throw away expired coupons?" There is a bit of truth in this, especially when you're throwing away a stack of 50 or 75 coupons that you painstakingly clipped a few months earlier. But think like a fisherman: you can whine about the ones that got away, or you can revel in the ones that you caught. It's all just part of the process. And remember: there is no way for you to know which items will be on special at your grocery store in three or four weeks. The coupon that you didn't clip might be the one that you wished you had later on…

## Big Idea Recap – Chapter 8

*BIG IDEA 49: Coupons work just like currency at the cash register. THERE IS NO DIFFERENCE. If you're throwing away the coupons from your Sunday paper, you're throwing away cash.*

*BIG IDEA 50: Unless you're an industry insider or a psychic, you don't know what's going to be on sale at your store in three or four weeks. The coupon you don't clip because you "can't afford that brand" could have made that item cheaper than the store brand on your next shopping trip.*

# Chapter 9:  Clubs, Cards & Counterintelligence

**FREQUENT SHOPPER CARDS: Value, with a price.**

As any astute shopper knows, the only way to get the lowest prices in the grocery store is to join the store's frequent shopper club program. You sign up for the program at the Customer Service counter, and typically they give you a plastic sheet with a punch-out membership card and a couple of punch out key fobs. All of these items feature a barcode, and the barcode identifies you to the store's computer every time you shop there.  In most stores, the ONLY way you can get the 'sale' prices on the items is to be a member of their shopping club.

**<u>You must join every club, at every store you shop in – even if you only shop there once or twice per year.</u>**

Why?  Because you will save money immediately and instantly every time you shop.

Here's how these clubs work:

**1. JOIN.**  You join the club.
**2. SHOP.**  Look for the special discount signs on products throughout the store. They will typically show two prices: A. the regular price, and B. the club member's price.
**3. SCAN.**  When you go to check out, you present your card or your key fob to the cashier. The cashier will scan the barcode on the card or key fob, and the computer will instantly recognize you as a club member. You will receive the club member discount price on the featured items.
**4. GET ANALYZED.**  What the store DOESN'T tell you (or at best, minimally tells you) is that their system is collecting information on your family's purchasing habits and product preferences. They sell this information to data compilers and marketing firms. Often, a store makes more money by selling this information than they do on the products you have purchased!

Why is your information so valuable?  The truth is individual family information is not extremely valuable by itself. But as a member of a specific demographic group, your data can help identify trends and validate information that is VERY profitable to the grocery product industry. For example, let's say that your household income is between $75,000 and $80,000, your age is 35 to 40 and you have 3 children under the age of 10. You are a powerhouse consumer, and the grocery industry wants you to buy the smallest packages of the most expensive brands at the highest prices. They are committed to influencing you to shop this way, so they make the most money off of you.

**"Big Brother" is alive and well; he's hiding in the aisles of your grocery store.**

Here's something else that few shoppers know: consumer product manufacturers pay stores a 'slot fee' for the space on their shelves. That is why a national brand gets the middle shelves that are at eye level, and the discount store brands get the bottom shelves. The national brands pay the highest shelf fees, because they know that most consumers are lazy and will buy the first product that they see in the category they are shopping for. This translates into huge sales and huge revenues for the manufacturers.

Let's say for example that the store features a national brand of cookies at a special rate, i.e. '2 for $3.99', when the normal price of a single item is $2.19. Of course, they will monitor the sales of this item by the total number of items sold. BUT – they will also be monitoring the demographics of the people purchasing them. If they find that families with your demographic indicators participate in this pricing offer 45% more than families with lower incomes, they will realize that they DO NOT have to lower the price of this product below this point to maintain market share. They will have learned that their target audience – affluent young families with children – are perfectly happy to buy two units at a total savings of 39¢ – and there is no need to offer a lower price point or a 'Buy one / get one free' package deal. The market will have spoken loud and clear and saved the manufacturer a ton of money in promoting that specific product.

The buying patterns of shoppers at your local grocery store often dictate the prices you will pay. If shoppers are lazy and prove that they will pay any cost for a particular item, they are in essence telling the store manager, "PLEASE RAISE OUR PRICES!" And guess what? The manager will gladly comply...

This is all a long way of saying that discount clubs will save you money every time you shop. You need to join them. But the main purpose of these clubs is not to save you money, although they will. The real goal behind these clubs is something... well.... slightly more sinister.

**Welcome to the Maze.**

If you've ever thought that the aisles in your grocery store can seem like a rat maze in a testing laboratory, you're not too far off the mark, *(ever notice that they ALWAYS keep the cheese in the back of the store...?)* The truth of the matter is that shoppers' clubs are the ultimate tool used by the food industry to make you a walking, talking participant in the world's largest focus group. As a club member, just about every purchase you make is being monitored, recorded and analyzed for future use by marketing firms. Now, before you get shocked or scared or decide to quit the shopper's club (a truly BAD idea), let's look at how this happens:

**1. REGISTRATION.** To get your discount card or key tag that entitles you to discounts at the store, you have to fill out a registration form. You tell them your name, street address, etc. They may ask you for some demographic information such as your age, marital status, children's age, etc. Most of this information is available from national consumer databases anyway.

**2. PRODUCT CODE.** Every item in the store carries a product code; you can see it below the barcode on the package. Every different size / shape / flavor has a unique code that is captured when the check-out clerk scans the package. The computer knows what every item is, in infinite detail; you can't keep any secrets from the grocery store's computer.

**3. CLUB MEMBER CODE.** That little store tag you keep on your key chain has a barcode, too. Guess what product that code represents? It's YOU. The computer knows who you are, where you live, and what you buy. But it doesn't know that you like to sneak out and get a pint of premium ice cream on a Saturday night, does it? No, no, no...

Of course it DOES know that your household consumes 1.4 bottles of Italian salad dressing per month, compared to your neighbor across the street whose family consumes 2.1 bottles per month. It knows that you have tried the store brand dressing once, but prefer the name brand variety. It knows that you got crazy last November and tried the balsamic vinaigrette but it probably wasn't a hit because you didn't buy it again. And it knows that you tried a competing grocery chain in August because the 1.4 bottle level dropped to 0.6 that month. Scary stuff, huh? And that's just the tip of the iceberg lettuce....

**4. SHARED DATA.** If your grocery store chain knows all of these intimate details about your household, surely they're keeping it private – aren't they??? Well, in a word, NO. In fact, they'll sell it to just about anyone who wants it. Why would they do this to you, their loyal customer? This information is worth BIG BUCKS to people in the industry, people whose job is to SELL YOU MORE STUFF! Information is money and time is money. The information saves them time, so they can get to the ultimate solution faster. The ultimate solution being, getting you to buy more stuff at a higher price and consume it faster. So if manufacturer "A" has a wealth of information on the salad dressing preferences in a particular metropolitan area, manufacturer "B" may 'cut to the chase' quicker by purchasing this information. They can save a year or more of expensive research time, and they can reap this data to sell more of THEIR product using the data.

But wait a minute – isn't it true that the affluent neighborhoods sell more of everything at a higher price, so the manufacturers just focus on THOSE markets? Why would they mess with the many lower or middle-income neighborhoods in the nation? Actually, this falls under the category of 'picking the lowest-hanging fruit first'. And these guys know all about the low-hanging fruit. They've picked it, packaged it, shipped it, and sold it for years. But if you view the nation as a giant pyramid based on affluence, the top 1/10th of that pyramid is the affluent markets. The bottom 90% of the pyramid is the lower to middle-income neighborhoods. Based on sheer numbers, the majority of the profit for these food manufacturers is found in the secondary markets and lower.

SIMPLY PUT: you may live in Podunk, but the information on your buying habits is just as important – and possibly even MORE important – than the buying habits of rich people on Rodeo Drive. You're part of a larger consumer group. EVERY consumer in America is of interest to the food manufacturers, not just the wealthiest households.

**5. GOOD DATA = GOOD VALUES.** The good part of this whole process is that you are proving your worth to the food industry with every purchase you make. To see how this works, let's look at a fictitious customer "Betty" who lives in a smaller rural city.

Betty doesn't make a huge income, but she's doing alright. Her kids seem to like "Fruit Goop" cereal, because she's buying 4.7 boxes per month – and not the smaller boxes, but the big family-size boxes. The manufacturers of "Berry Blop" cereal are envious, and they'd sure like Betty to migrate over to their brands. After all, if they can figure out how to get her to switch brands and become a loyal customer of theirs, they can use the same technique to influence the 15.3 million other shoppers like Betty who live in similar-size communities and make similar levels of income.

So Betty starts getting some really interesting coupons in the mail or through the internet *(see the online coupon section at the end of this book.)* These values can help Betty really save some cash, if only she would try them. So Betty redeems the coupon and brings the cereal home, and lo and behold – the kids could care less whether they're eating Fruit Goop or Berry Blop. So the kids are happy, Betty's happy because she saved a lot of cash, and the food manufacturer is happy because he's successfully migrated Betty away from Fruit Goop. But the story doesn't end there…

The manufacturers of Fruit Goop cereal notice that Betty's volume – a steady 4.7 boxes for the past 3 years – has dwindled to…. ZERO

BOXES! Flashing red lights and alarms are going off in the factory. "Something must be done," shouts the big boss with the cigar in his mouth. And so the legions of marketers snap into action and start blitzing Betty with huge discounts on Fruit Goop cereal. So now she can redeem these coupons on Fruit Goop and save even more money. The kids, meanwhile, are mass-consuming whatever she pours into their bowls. They're oblivious. Betty is ecstatic; her monthly food bills are going down. But wait, there's more...

The manufacturer of Berry Blop notices that he's losing out again. He redoubles his effort – issuing even more coupons for the brand that he knows Betty's brood prefers two to one over Fruit Goop. So Betty uses those coupons on her next shopping trip. Repeat this cycle over and over, until the Betty clan outgrows their preference for excessively-sugared products, and wakes up to real nutrition. Then, the manufacturers start in on her new neighbors who have younger kids...

While cynical and exaggerated, the example of "Betty" above is the basic process of couponing in America today. And while the delivery vehicles are not always so targeted, the industry is headed more and more in this direction. Take note of the coupons that are printed at the cash register: these are the principal ammunition in the household preference wars. Some coupons are printed and delivered directly to the household, but these are on a more infrequent basis due to the high cost. The biggest volume of activity in these wars takes place on a market-by-market level. The industry looks at overall performance by select demographic groups, and responds to the market as a whole by varying the coupon amounts and promotional activity by individual market. This is far more prevalent than individual household couponing. But the industry is getting more household-centric as technology gets more advanced. And certain changes in our technology-savvy households are closer than you think...

**6. GUESS WHO'S COMING TO (TV) DINNER?** *(Apologies to Spencer Tracy, Sidney Poitier and Katharine Hepburn).* Did you know that over-the-air TV broadcast is ending in 2009? More and more households are buying High Definition TV sets (HDTV), and soon everyone will have a digital receiver (or 2, 3, 4 or more) in their household. The color and clarity will be fantastic. The number and diversity of the channels will be spectacular. And the commercials? Well, they'll be aimed directly between your eyes, or more specifically – your wallet.

Let's say your name is Suzy Shopper and your neighbor across the street is Charlie Consumer, and you're both watching the latest chapter of "Desperate Cowgirls", the #1 network show far and wide. When it goes to commercial, you – Suzy Shopper – are viewing a commercial for the latest gas-guzzling vehicle to sputter out of Detroit. That's because you're driving a seven year old import, and your index potential for a new car purchase in the next six months is off the charts. Your neighbor Charlie, meanwhile, is viewing a commercial for golf clubs, because he plays golf six times a month.

Hey – wait a minute – how did they know he's a golfer and I'm driving an old car??? And how the heck did they change those commercials out between our two households…??? This is simple stuff with the new technology in place today. And as far as knowing your lifestyle / hobbies / major purchases and brand preference? Heck, they even know what brand toothpaste you use…

So how does this relate to you, Suzy Shopper and Charlie Consumer, each snug in your little condos in front of your blazing hot wide-screen Plasma HDTVs? The marketers are coming for you both – individually and personally – and they're out for nothing less than total mind control. Okay, that sounded a little out there even for me… but the truth is that your buying habits are being monitored and addressed on increasingly-specific levels.

The war for your wallet is gearing up for high speed, high-tech battle. And in the grand scheme of things, you are powerless to stop it. Sure, you can TiVo your way out of the commercials. But guess what? Soon enough, you won't WANT to. And here's why:

Here you are, Suzy Shopper, watching the Cowgirls prance across your screen. Before you can grab the remote, a commercial for the new "MegaSmog V8 convertible" comes across your screen, and the graphic says, "Suzy – we'll pay you $100 to test drive this car today!" And you're thinking, "WOW – I could really use that $100 to buy 5 gallons of gas for my current car, but I'm never going to buy a new car; I'll just go down there and get my free cash!"

So you go down to the dealership, and you get your $100. The dealer is happy, too, because he knows that you are an interested shopper. He will continue to target you until you finally convert and buy the new car. It's a numbers game, so he's just happy to move you up the priority ladder among prospects.

Meanwhile, your neighbor Charlie was previously watching Desperate Cowgirls, but he got bored and switched over to the Knitting Network. Guess what? The commercials followed him over there. In the future (i.e. now, or thereabouts), advertisers will buy time by households, segmented by very precise demographic indicators, rather than by blocks of time on a network. So whatever channel you select, you'll get a certain amount of household-specific offers.

So Charlie is watching "Knit One / Purl, Too!" – on the Knitting Network, his favorite hobby channel, and up comes a commercial for the latest set of golf clubs from Wham-Co. Charlie is perfectly happy with his old set of clubs, but the ad says, "Hey Charlie – come to Gargantuan Golf World this weekend, and we'll give you a dozen balls free – just for testing our new clubs." Charlie was headed there to pick up some new balls anyway, so he says "what the heck" and heads off to the store. Soon thereafter, he's on the driving range blasting away with his new set of Wham-Co clubs, which, as he discovered at the store, he simply could not live without…

**THE MORAL OF THE STORY:** It's really quite simple: whether you are a prospect for a new car, a set of golf clubs, or a year's supply of Fruit Goop cereal, your shopping selections are VERY IMPORTANT to manufacturers today. If you learn how to play their game and work their system, you can enjoy some real values and real savings.

You may scoff at grocery coupons today. But coupons are coming your way, even if you never open the Sunday newspaper or read your mail: they will simply be delivered electronically. And you will WANT to view them and redeem them.

The firms that purchase your family's shopping habits and brand preferences from your local grocery store are doing it now, and they will continue to do it in the future. Much of this data originates from the lowly-little 'frequent shopper club' tag sitting on your key chain. Is this whole process a bad thing or a good thing? Well, you DO end up saving money when you use the club card, so there are immediate benefits to you that can help your family's budget.

Are there long-term disadvantages? That is a debatable subject, and the truth is that this process will go on very well without you, thank you. You're really not helping any cause or righting any wrongs by NOT participating in the program. The decision to join the club or not join the club is a personal one, so make an informed decision for you and your family that matches your personal preferences and comfort levels. But in my book, getting the most for your shopping dollar is first and foremost. So I don't have any problem in recommending shopping club membership to everyone.

## Big Idea Recap – Chapter 9

*BIG IDEA 51: If you "don't have time" to sign up for the grocery store shopper's club, you "don't have time" to save money. Affix a "sucker" label to your forehead and tell people proudly that you pay full price, every day, for every item in the store.*

*BIG IDEA 52: "Big Brother" is alive and well; he's hiding in the aisles of your grocery store. If you are a member of a frequent-shopper club, be aware that every purchase you make – or don't make – is being monitored. There is really no down side to this or personal repercussions, but you need to know that you're part of one of the world's largest focus groups of all time.*

*BIG IDEA 53: The buying patterns of shoppers at your local grocery store often dictate the prices you will pay. If shoppers are lazy and prove that they will pay any cost for a particular item, they are in essence telling the store manager, "PLEASE RAISE OUR PRICES!" And guess what? The manager will gladly comply...*

*BIG IDEA 54: Get a frequent shopper cart at every grocery store you visit, even if you only shop there once or twice a year; the bargains are well worth it.*

**BIG IDEA 55:** *Concerned about privacy? Register using your work address, or a P.O. Box. You'll still get the card and enjoy the discounts, but it will be harder for the store to link this to your home address. Of course, you'll have to pay with cash because they can get your address off your check or your credit/ debit card.*

**BIG IDEA 56:** *EVERY consumer in America is of interest to the food manufacturers, not just the wealthiest households. The shopping actions of a lower-income household are monitored just as closely as those of the most affluent households.*

**BIG IDEA 57:** *The more coupons you redeem, the more interest you will attract from food marketers. You'll get more offers and better values over time. The sooner you start the process, the sooner you'll get into the higher discount levels.*

**BIG IDEA 58:** *Today's brand marketers know a LOT about you already. If you learn how to play their game, you can enjoy increasing amounts of free stuff, discounts and special values that other people won't enjoy.*

**BIG IDEA 59:** *You may scoff at grocery coupons today. But coupons are coming your way, even if you never open the Sunday newspaper or read your mail: they will simply be delivered electronically. And you will WANT to view them and redeem them, because you'll get lots of free stuff and better deals on virtually everything you buy – even cars, HDTV sets, cell phones and other high-ticket items.*

**BIG IDEA 60:** *Sign up for frequent shopper clubs at every grocery store you visit. If you're traveling on vacation and need groceries, get a card at the grocery store in that area, even if you don't plan to return anytime soon; you'll get the card immediately, and you could save $10 or $20 just on your one visit.*

# Chapter 10: The Power of Rebate Clubs, aka "Your Check's in the Mail"

### *Why you should join every one you can.*

What is a rebate club? Simply put, it is an ongoing store promotion that lets you purchase items and get some or all of the purchase price back in the form of a cash rebate. These are typically found at the larger drug store chains, which issue a monthly flyer of offers. My record on free items is $62 in one month, and every item was something that somebody in my family could use.

When it comes to pharmacies, people are definitely creatures of habit. The store that you use to get your prescriptions filled is generally the store that you get your drug store supplies from. It's not always true, because some people get their prescriptions at the food store, but people do tend to have their #1 favorite in terms of where they buy their shampoo, hair coloring, toupee wax, etc. *(Does anyone use toupee wax anymore? There's a question for the ages...)* So if you're like most people, you rarely – if ever – venture over to the 'brand X' pharmacy. Here's a money-saving tip: wander over there at least once a month, just to pick up their rebate club flyer.

Visit all the major drug store chain stores in your area at least once a month, even if you don't normally shop there. The rebate club offers can allow you to get as much as $50 in FREE merchandise each month. If you visit 3 stores a month, you could literally get $150 in FREE stuff each month – up to $1,800 a year. Even if you're not super-diligent or the offers aren't that lucrative every month of the year, this one technique alone could save you over $1,000 a year on drug store supplies!

It's no secret that the pharmacy chains are in big competition with each other, so most of the big chains offer rebate clubs. The target for these clubs is not the income-earning, hard-working youth of America; it's the seniors. Seniors spend more per capita on prescriptions than any other demographic group. The store doesn't care about giving $20 or $30 in rebate money to a senior, when they're going to buy $200 or $300 in prescriptions each month. I have found that some national chains offer the rebate club in all markets, but in some tourist destinations you have to ask the cashier for a copy of the rebate book. Apparently, they don't want tourists with disposable cash to get a break on anything – especially if they're ready to pay full price without question. Or it could be that they only want to offer the book to seniors, because they don't want low-dollar customers to take advantage of the rebates. The truth is that the stores cannot legally exclude any individual from getting the rebates. You may be a struggling young family with a little cash in the bank but you are entitled to get the rebates just like anyone else.

Here's how rebate club programs typically work:

**1. GET THE REBATE BOOK OR FLYER.** In most drug stores, the flyer is on a rack as you enter the store.

**2. REVIEW THE OFFERS.** You will typically find items that are offered with a 100% rebate, i.e. a $7.99 bottle of sun tan lotion with a $7.99 rebate for buying it. Others will be $1.00, $2.00 or $3.00 off the purchase price of the item. You have to check these carefully, because some manufacturers will offer a $3.00 rebate on a $2.99 item; it's really free, but they don't want people buying it just because of that. This is a subtle way by which they try to discourage the 'freebie' nuts that will take anything for free – even if they don't want or need it. *(HINT: be a 'freebie' nut.)*

**3. CHECK THE OFFER DATES.** It's critical that you check the valid dates of the offer. One major drug store chain that will go unnamed has started to stagger their rebate offers throughout the month, but they only tell you this in the fine print. In other words, the first free item may earn you a 100% rebate, but you must buy it between the first and 7th of the month; the next item may also give you a 100% rebate, but you have to purchase it between the 8th and 16th of the month. They're trying to encourage repeat visits, but it's really more trouble than it's worth, unless you are super-diligent and/or a frequent visitor to that store anyway.

**4. MAIL IN THE REBATE REQUEST.** Be sure to process your

rebate request and mail it off IMMEDIATELY when you get home. Here's a rule that works for me: I don't allow myself to put the products away until I have completed the rebate forms AND sealed the envelope. What you DON'T want to do is say, "I'll do it later" – because out of sight is out of mind, and most people will surely forget to do the paperwork – thus, they lose their rebate – and that is what the drug store chains are counting on. The sad truth is that a very high percentage of people who intend to mail in their rebate requests never quite get around to it. The retailers call this "breakage", and they are counting on you to procrastinate. If you want to be sure you get every extra dollar that's coming to you, don't procrastinate: set a filing procedure that works for you and stick to it.

**5. READ THE REQUIREMENTS.** Some rebates require that you cut out the barcode off the product, or write the product's barcode number down on your rebate form. Read the fine print, because some of these stores will deny you the rebate if you don't do everything they say, exactly the way they say it.

**6. CHECK THE POSTMARK DATE REQUIREMENTS.** Another critical item is the postmark date on your mail-in rebate request. For most clubs, if you are responding to a January Rebate Club offer, your mail-in request MUST be postmarked by February 5th, or they will refuse it. Think you can 'slide'? Don't count on it. The stores really don't want to give you the rebate, so they'll use any and all excuses not to issue the rebate check. I was once denied a $50 rebate check because the store's cash register didn't date the receipt. How does a cash register malfunction and not print the date? It's beyond me, but you can bet that I called them out on it and eventually got my rebate. How did I do it? I had back-up ammunition, which is the next critical point.

**7. KEEP A PHOTO COPY.** Some of the less-scrupulous clubs or their 3rd party vendors will try to get around sending you a rebate check. It's a good practice to photocopy everything and keep in a file. After a few months, if you haven't gotten your rebate, you'll have proof of mailing it in. SIDE NOTE: if you are allowed to use your company postage meter, you can photocopy your outer envelope with the postmark date. That gives you positive proof that you mailed it within the proper timeframe. This may seem like a lot of work, but on more than one occasion I have had a rebate processing company deny my rebate claiming that I violated rule X. Using my photocopies, I've gone to the store manager and pointed out that I did everything I was asked to. The store managers have always made good on the rebate offers, and simply turned my photocopies in to their regional managers. It may seem trivial, but if you're denied a $50 or greater rebate like I was, it becomes your word against theirs – and having a back-up plan can help settle the dispute in your favor.

**8. BUG 'EM IF THEY'RE LATE.** Don't be afraid to call the rebate company if they're late mailing you a check. Some companies intentionally do not mail rebate checks unless the consumer calls to complain. They're counting on a large number of respondents simply forgetting about it, which saves the rebate company a lot of cash. And I wouldn't be shocked if the third party processing companies turn in 100% of the rebate requests to the retailer, but only mail out checks to a small portion of the consumers. Proving this would be difficult, but that's not my concern: I just want what's coming to me, and a well-timed call to a 1-800-number can often get you quick service on your rebate request.

**9. USE THE STORE'S GIFT CARD PLAN.** Some stores use a magnetic stripe gift card to provide rebate funds. It's cheaper for them than issuing checks. Plus, one major chain offers you a 10% 'bump' in your rebate total if you'll allow them to post the rebate amount to your rechargeable gift card, rather than have them issue you a check. It's a handy way to get a little extra cash back. Plus, it's a huge kick to buy the next month's freebies with a gift card, so you're actually getting more free stuff without spending any actual cash…

**10. USE YOUR GIFT CARD'S STORED VALUE FIRST, CASH SECOND.** If your store puts your rebate amount on a gift card, use it first when making purchases at the store, then pay any remaining balance with cash. You don't earn interest by keeping the value on the card, and you can't turn it in for cash. So always use the credit before using real cash; it's good money management.

The downside of rebate clubs is that your cash is tied up for 30 to 60 days while your rebate form is being processed. Sorry – there is no way around this one. If you are really cash-strapped, I would suggest putting the purchases on a credit card. Then, when the rebate check arrives, deposit it and IMMEDIATELY write a check in the exact amount to your credit card company. You only have to do this once, if you do it right. You can use the rebate amount to purchase the next month's rebate items.

Rebate clubs give you money back on everyday items that you're probably buying already, many of which are only available from a pharmacy and not a dollar store. Since you need them and are going to buy them anyway – regardless of the cost – it's well worth your time to apply for and get all the rebates that are available.

## The Most Amazing, Well-Hidden Drug Store Shopping Secret.

Another secret about shopping at the big-box drug stores that you may never have heard of is the availability of multiple coupon redemption. In most grocery stores, presenting a second coupon for a single item will cause the cash register to error out. Alarms will go off, the secret 'coupon police' in dark suits with sunglasses will come rushing in, and you'll be pinned to the floor with an AK47 pointed at your forehead. Well, that may be a little bit exaggerated, but you get the point: double-coupon presentment is fraud, and the stores don't like it and won't accept it. Why is it, then, that some drug stores not only accept it but ENCOURAGE it? It's true!

A recent flyer in my Sunday newspaper showed a $3.00 store coupon issued by the retailer, good on a select manufacturer's brand of soaps and shampoos: buy any 3 and get $3.00 off. The headline read, "Save even more with manufacturer coupons found in today's paper." In checking the other coupons, I found a $2.00 off coupon on one brand of shampoo, and $1.00 off coupons on several others. So I could easily get a total of $8.00 off on three brand-name products! There are several things you should be aware of, however:

• **No Doubling.** Most drug stores do NOT double coupons like the grocery stores do. (No big deal here, because stores in my area only double up to 50¢ – one up to 99¢ – and these coupons were all above that value.)

• **No Price Reductions.** When the drug store puts out savings like this, the items are usually priced at full retail value – so you're starting from the highest price-point possible.

All that said, however, the savings are still well worth the effort of claiming them. Saving $8.00 on a total purchase price of $14 for three items is a bargain among bargains – you end up paying $2.00 per item for premium products – in this case hair care items. And if you have teenagers in the family whose entire world revolves around hair volume, bounce and shine – getting premium products makes all the difference in the world.

## Big Idea Recap – Chapter 10

*BIG IDEA 61: Visit all of the major drug store chain stores in your area at least once a month, even if you don't normally shop there. The rebate club offers can allow you to get as much as $50 in FREE merchandise each month. If you visit 3 stores a month, you could literally get $150 in FREE stuff each month – up to $1,800 a year. Even if you're not super-diligent or the offers aren't that lucrative every month of the year, this one technique alone could save you over $1,000 a year on drug store supplies!*

*BIG IDEA 62: Rebate clubs give you money back on everyday items that you're probably buying already, many of which are only available from a pharmacy and not a dollar store. Since you need them and are going to buy them anyway – regardless of the cost – it's well worth your time to apply for and get all of the rebates that are available.*

*BIG IDEA 63: Some drug store chains will let you redeem both STORE coupons and MANUFACTURER coupons for the same item, at the same time. It gives you a double-whammy of savings and often makes it possible for you to buy the super-premium brands at a price that is less than the 'bargain' no-name products!*

# Chapter 11: A Rebate Returned is Money Earned

**INDIVIDUAL PRODUCT OR BRAND REBATES:** Are they worth the effort? YES!!!

One way that manufacturers attempt to boost the sales of their entire product line is to offer a cash back deal when you buy a certain number of their products. A typical example is "$5 cash back when you buy 10 of your favorites!" The ad will show a photo of the items you have to buy to get the rebate. As always – there are details and conditions you have to know, so be sure you follow them so you'll actually get the rebate check in the mail rather than a "we're sorry" notice. Here are some of the 'secrets' of gaining the best value with a rebate, using the 'buy 10' offer as an example. Remember that this offer gives you back $0.50 per item purchased, minus the cost of the envelope and stamp to mail it back in.

**1. READ THE FINE PRINT.** Okay, so this one is obvious. But instead of just giving the fine print a cursory glance, read it, and understand it BEFORE you shop – or you could be out of qualification for the rebate money. The offer may require that you send in the original cash register receipt for each of the 10 items, circling each of the ten on the receipt. They may require a certain size / flavor / packaging of the product *(12 oz. cans of Fizzy-Soda may not qualify if the coupon specifically requires that you buy 16 oz. bottles of Fizzy-Soda.)* There may be a date limit to your purchase, so you can't use last week's receipt if the starting date is from this week's newspaper. Also, the offer may require that you mail in the original coupon and not use a photocopy or printout off a rebate website. Another key thing to watch is the quantity per individual item that is allowed. In one case, you could buy up to two of any particular item – any more of that item did not count toward the ten-item minimum.

**2. LOOK AT THE PHOTO.** The fine print may say that the offer is good on a particular brand of product, but the photo may show a certain flavor or packaging style of that product. Unless the fine print specifically says that all sizes and flavors qualify, assume that their intention is that you buy the one shown in the photo.

**3. LOOK AT WHAT'S <u>NOT</u> IN THE PHOTO.** A little detective work can often greatly increase the value you get from the rebate. In one example, the photo shows the higher-priced items – kids-size yogurt tubes, yogurt drinks, kids' fruit snacks, meal helper mixes – mostly the highest-priced items in the offer. Other products are listed in the fine print as qualifying for the offer, but they're not shown in the photo. See if you can guess why these items weren't shown: soup, canned vegetables and their entire line of Mexican food products. Here's why:

*a. The soup line is already heavily couponed, meaning you can find coupons for these items every day in numerous places.*

*b. The Mexican food line is also heavily couponed, plus they have many lower cost items like refried beans which are often priced at less than $1.00 per can.*

*c. While the name brand canned vegetables are typically more expensive than the store brands, they're also on sale quite frequently, and you can also find coupons for them from time to time.*

To get the maximum value for your effort, your mission should be to purchase the 10 lowest-price items that will qualify for the offer, and use coupons when purchasing as many of the 10 items as possible. Here's why:

| Item Cost | Retail Price | Savings With Doubled Coupons | Rebate Amount On This Item | Net Cost of Item After Rebate Only (No Coupons) | Net Cost of Item After Rebate AND Coupons |
|---|---|---|---|---|---|
| Cereal A | $3.99 | $1.10 (55¢ coupon) | $0.50 | $3.49 | $2.39 |
| 'Helper' Meal Mix | $2.59 | $0.70 (35¢ coupon) | $0.50 | $2.09 | $1.39 |
| Yogurt in a Tube | $3.59 | $1.10 (55¢ coupon) | $0.50 | $3.09 | $1.99 |
| Baking Mix | $3.39 | $1.00 (50¢ coupon) | $0.50 | $2.89 | $1.89 |
| Frozen Waffle Sticks | $3.89 | $0.80 (40¢ coupon) | $0.50 | $3.39 | $2.59 |
| Can Green Beans - Quantity 2 | $1.78 ($0.89 each) | $0.70 (35¢ coupon) | $1.00 (qty. 2) | $0.78 | $0.08 |
| Frozen Carrots | $1.49 | $0.70 (35¢ coupon) | $0.50 | $0.99 | $0.29 |
| Biscuits in a Tube | $1.59 | $1.10 (55¢ coupon) | $0.50 | $1.09 | ($0.01) |
| Croissants in a Tube | $1.99 | $1.10 (55¢ coupon) | $0.50 | $1.49 | $0.39 |
| **FINAL COST** | **$24.30** | - | - | **$19.30** | **$11.00** |
| *TOTAL SAVINGS* | *$0* | *($8.30)* | - | *($5.00)* | *($13.30)* |

As you can see, the rebate was a good deal to begin with – by itself it saved you almost 26% on the groceries. But if you use the coupons in combination with the rebate, you'll save _**over 45%**_ on the same groceries!

## Big Idea Recap – Chapter 11

*BIG IDEA 64: There's no doubt about it: mail-in rebates are a real pain in the neck, due to all of the paperwork you have to complete. The manufacturers are counting on you NOT to make the effort. But if you DO make the effort, you can save an extra $10, $20 or $30 a month on groceries. It doesn't sound like much, but this one technique can generate $100 to $300 per year in savings: it's like getting your groceries FREE for 1 or 2 weeks out of the year.*

# Chapter 12: The Economics of Food

## *Grocery Selections = Operating Margin*

In the restaurant business – as in any business – the difference between the COST OF THE INGREDIENTS and the SALE PRICE of the prepared food item is called the MARGIN. This margin of profitability determines how much PROFIT the restaurant will make at the end of the day. This is the primary reason that chefs look for the lowest-cost provider of the CORE ingredients they use in their restaurant. *(Note that this is DIFFERENT from the FEATURED ingredients or SPECIALTY items).* We're talking about flour, dairy products, spices, etc. – items they use each and every day. Restaurants must maintain their budgets and a high level of profit margin, if they are to remain viable and profitable. Your home budget has a MARGIN as well. Learning how to control your margin can make a huge difference in how well your family lives.

For an example, let's look at a fictitious family. The Jones family earns a salary of $36,500 per year after taxes, for an even average take-home amount of $100 per day. Here's how this $100 per day is spent:

**Mortgage: 35%**
**Utilities: 10%**
**Home Maintenance: 5%**
**Insurance / Health Care: 10%**
**Clothing / Personal: 10%**
**Auto: 5%**
**Savings / Retirement: 5%**
**Food / Entertainment: 20%**
**TOTAL: 100%**

This family's budget for food and entertainment is $20 per day. This gives them a total spending allotment of $600 per month. Assuming that the Jones family eats every breakfast and dinner at home, and 'brown bags' their lunches, they can spend a total of $150 per week at the grocery store, or a total of $21.43 per day on meals.

The MARGIN for the Jones family is whether they can actually feed their family on $21.43 per day, or whether they will need to take money away from the other budgeted items to meet their grocery bill.

At a restaurant, the MARGIN determines whether the establishment will show a profit at the end of the month or not. Often, the area that must give way is the owner's paycheck. If the restaurant doesn't show a profit, the owner doesn't get a paycheck. If the restaurant consistently fails to create a margin of profit, the business will fail.

At the Jones household, if the food expenditure exceeds the budgeted 20%, the family must do without new clothing, reduce or eliminate their savings, cancel their insurance, or reduce in one of the other areas. If the family's total expenditure consistently outstrips their income, the family budget will fail and the family will eventually declare bankruptcy or lean on parents or other relatives to bail them out financially.

This is why it is important to stretch your family budget as much as possible, and why the choices you make at the grocery store CAN and WILL impact all areas of your family's life. So let's take a look at smart choices you can make to get the absolute most out of your grocery dollar.

Operate your home kitchen the same way that a professional chef operates their kitchen: as a business. Every item that you can buy for less will IMPROVE your operating margin; every item that you pay full price for will DETRACT from your operating margin. The success of your family's annual budget depends on staying within or below your budgetary margin consistently, month after month.

## Big Idea Recap – Chapter 12

*BIG IDEA 65: Operate your home kitchen the same way that a professional chef operates his or her kitchen: as a business. Every item that you can buy for less will IMPROVE your operating margin; every item that you pay full price for will DETRACT from your operating margin. The success of your family's annual budget depends on staying within – or below – your budgetary margin consistently, month after month.*

# Chapter 13: Smart Grocery Choices & Core Ingredients

Let me start by saying that I'm not preaching here. I don't advocate going 'back to your roots' and only buying raw materials. Many writers have covered that territory, telling you that you only need to buy a sack of flour, some eggs, milk and a few ingredients and grow everything else in your backyard. That's nice if your cup of tea is cooking everything from scratch and tending a garden for two or three hours a day. That approach simply doesn't work if you have a full-time job, a social life, and/or kids in school. It doesn't fit too well with modern life, let's leave it at that. Most of us are lucky to find a half-hour to ourselves every other day, let alone tackle a return to an all-natural lifestyle. Most of us need or justifiably want the conveniences of prepared foods to reduce our time in the kitchen. Mom needs a break too, you know.

Another thing I'm not advocating is a change in your diet. If you want to change your diet, that's fine; go see your doctor, get some professional advice, and put a plan in place. I'm not a doctor, and frankly I don't care what foods you choose to buy or eat. What I hope to do here is give you some ideas on how to enjoy the foods you want to eat, while paying less for them. That's all.

There are <u>three major ways to cut your grocery bill</u>, totally apart from using coupons or obtaining store discounts. They are:

• **BUY BIG.** Get larger sizes of items, as long as you and your family can consume them before they expire or lose their freshness.

If you typically buy a small jar of peanut butter every two weeks, consider buying the big jar every 4 weeks. The big jar typically contains twice as much, but only costs about 40% to 50% more. This same rule of thumb applies to hundreds of everyday grocery items, household supplies and personal care items. You may be in the habit of buying the smallest item because you want the least-expensive item, but by selecting the smallest package you are probably paying more per ounce than if you bought the bigger package.

• **MAKE TIMELY BUYS.** Stock up when items are on sale. Again, as long as the items are not highly perishable or they have a fairly decent shelf life, invest in additional units of items when they are at their lowest cost. Put two or three of the item on your back shelf, even if you won't need them for six months or a year. As long as you will eventually consume the item, if it's available now at half the cost or below, stock up & save.

• **BUY BASIC.** Buy the core ingredients of recipes, rather than pre-assembled mixtures of core ingredients. Select according to your taste & dietary preferences. But buy the primary ingredients of recipes rather than the put-together final products. Currently, you may not use any of the following core ingredients in your food selections, but for most families they are already a core part of their diet – often without consciously selecting them:

- *Potatoes*
- *Onions*
- *Carrots*
- *Tomatoes*
- *Mixed Vegetables – Seasonal*
- *Rice*
- *Pasta*
- *Meats: chicken, beef, pork, etc.*
- *Alternative Core Ingredients: Tofu, Sweet Potatoes, Bulgar Wheat, Grits*

There is a middle ground between buying a prepared baking mixture and growing your own wheat. Find the logical middle ground that works for you and your schedule. Let's use a frozen all-in-one dinner mix as an example.

A frozen dinner mixture may contain bite-size nuggets of chicken, plus chopped broccoli, rice and sauce. A bag of this mixture probably costs about $5.00 to $6.00, and will sort of feed the average four-person family adequately, (unless you have teenagers and a 5 lb. bag of food is an appetizer...) That's not too bad, when you consider the cost of eating the same type of meal at a restaurant. But it's not the best you can do price-wise, and cooking the same meal from scratch could cost you less than half this much. How? Let's look at the core ingredients.

The pre-blended mixture contains roughly the following ingredients:

- *One to one and a half chicken breasts cut in pieces.*
- *Two or three cups of cooked rice*
- *Two or three cups of chopped, cooked broccoli*
- *One or two cooked carrots, sliced*
- *1/4 cup of soy sauce*
- *One or two garlic cloves, chopped*
- *Various spices in minute amounts*
- *Various preservatives and chemicals (sorry, had to mention this...)*

Sounds like a lot, doesn't it? You dump the contents of the bag into a saucepan, cook on low for about 10 minutes, and it's ready to serve. The quality of the food is reasonably acceptable, except there's usually not as much chicken as you would like. The broccoli and carrots are kind of mushy, because they were cooked a few months ago and frozen. And, the garlic isn't really zingy, because it was chopped, cooked and frozen a long time ago. So overall, it's an okay meal, but nothing to rave about. It's sustenance, and that's what dinnertime is all about, isn't it? PERISH THE THOUGHT! Dinnertime should be about enjoying your food, savoring the taste, color and smell of a fresh-cooked meal – that's the difference between simply eating and eating well.

### Are All Mixes Bad?  Of Course Not!

Now, am I saying that ALL pre-mixed dinners or boxes of pre-cooked side dishes are bad? NO – of course not! The food companies are not bad people, and they're not idiots, either. The vast majority of these pre-mixed food items are very high in quality, and you can save a lot of time and effort by using them. But just be aware that you are paying a price for this convenience. The cost difference between frozen / boxed / dehydrated vegetables and fresh vegetables is not always huge. In some cases, the fresh vegetables can actually be higher. But in combination with all of the other elements that go into a meal, starting from core ingredients will almost always be less expensive.

## Variety – and Pre-Mixed Foods – Can Be A GOOD Thing!

Some pre-mixed or prepared foods allow you to enjoy items you would rarely cook from scratch – if ever. For example, would you make fresh stuffing if you had to start with the bread and spices and mix it all yourself? Probably not. But with a box of ready-to-go stuffing mix, you can have fresh stuffing in about 5 or 10 minutes. Is it bad stuff? Well, it's made of bread and spices, so it's just about the same thing YOU would make, IF you were starting from scratch. WHICH you wouldn't ever do. So no – it's NOT bad stuff, it's actually pretty darned good stuff!

The moral of this story: many, many, many of these pre-mixed food products are very good, and they can save you a lot of time. All I'm suggesting here is that you buy them when they're on sale, and you have a coupon for them. Stock up on them when the pricing is right, so they'll be on hand when you need them. And in many cases, you can go back to the core ingredients and replicate these mixes with fresh ingredients, resulting in better quality for less money.

Just remember this: in most cases, when you buy pre-mixed / pre-seasoned / prepared meals, you are paying a HUGE mark-up for the service. The more you get back to basics in your meal preparation, the more you will lower your cost of food.

## Big Idea Recap – Chapter 13

*BIG IDEA 66: By using core ingredients to prepare your family's meals, you can reduce your total cost of food. Pre-packaged meals can cost up to 5 times as much as the same meal prepared from scratch. Develop a set of time-saving recipes that use core ingredients, and you can easily cut your food costs in HALF.*

*BIG IDEA 67: Generally speaking, the smaller the package – the greater the cost per ounce / pound. If you are cooking for one, or you eat like a church mouse, or the items you buy are very perishable, buying small makes sense. But for everyone / everything else, the bigger the package, the lower the cost per serving.*

**BIG IDEA 68:** *When you see a bargain, grab it. If it's a non-perishable item, grab 2 or 3 and stash them away for future use. You'll be investing a little cash now, but you'll be saving a lot of cash down the road.*

**BIG IDEA 69:** *Whenever you buy pre-mixed / pre-seasoned / prepared meals, you are paying a HUGE mark-up for the service. The more you get back to basics in your meal preparation, the more you will lower your cost of food.*

# Chapter 14: Real Food, Real Cooking

Let me be frank here: cooking is actually very, very simple. The greatest chefs in the world all cook the same way: they start with a core ingredient at the base and then they add something to it to make it unique. Many Italian dishes revolve around pasta; many middle-eastern dishes revolve around grains; many Chinese and Japanese dishes revolve around rice; many Irish dishes revolve around potatoes, and many Indian and southern Asian dishes revolve around a vegetable base.

Of course, some dishes are more elaborate and require multiple base items. Granted, there are exceptions to every rule. But the next time you are in your favorite restaurant, scan down the menu and count the dishes that are based on one core ingredient, and then count the dishes that have multiple core ingredients. You will be amazed at how simple the vast majority of dishes really are. With the majority of foods, simple is best: the basic flavor of the core ingredients is pure, simple, and delicious. A few minor enhancements can do wonders, of course, but deep down basic food is pretty darn good to begin with!

**Example: a carrot.** It rarely needs any improvement. Cook it until tender, and it's wonderful on the palate. Yes, you might add a little butter or tiny touch of brown sugar, but overall it's incredibly packed with flavor – right out of the ground.

**Example: a tomato.** Don't get me started. Tomatoes are so flavor-packed; they're tremendous in a million different ways. Add a touch of seasoning and they're on just about everyone's top-10 list.

**Example: a potato.** Cook them, fry them, whip them, sauté them – you can do a 1,001 things with a potato. They are wonderfully complex yet simple at the same time. A little enhancement can make a world of difference, but you can't improve on the pure nutrition that is built into the spud.

You really don't have to do a lot of fancy cooking to make good food when you start with nature's finest. It's hard to top perfection.

Okay, I know you're thinking: "I'm too busy to cook, I have to use pre-made mixes, I don't have time to cook". And yes, you have a valid point. We're all too busy these days to even think about cooking, let alone crack open the recipe book. I want to change the way you think about cooking. If you can change your mindset about core ingredients and what it MEANS to cook, you'll discover that it simply doesn't have to be that difficult.

The food industry WANTS you to think that cooking is difficult, so you'll buy their pre-cooked meals. If people knew how easy it is to cook from scratch – at a fraction of the price of buying their pre-packaged meals – they wouldn't make as much money.

Think of how many commercials you've seen where the wife heats up a ready-to-eat dish of pre-mixed stuff, and the family goes wild with glee at the wonderful taste and nutrition. *(And by the way, why is it always the WIFE? We husbands cook, too!)* They always show how the preparation takes just a minute or two, and the end results are always perfect. THIS IS BRAINWASHING, PEOPLE! They are conditioning you to think that COOKING = HARD WORK and PAIN. BUYING THEIR MIX = SIMPLICITY and COMFORT.

**Wean yourself from the notion that cooking is difficult.** Cooking can be one of the simplest things in your life, if you approach it correctly. It's the key to seriously reducing your food budget, too.

In reality, cooking from scratch (or at least using a few core ingredients) can be JUST AS EASY. To make my point, here are five dinners you can cook in LESS THAN FIVE MINUTES (and actually less than 1 minute if you're fast...)

**1. BAKED POTATO.** Take a potato. Wash it off. Poke holes in it with a fork. Shake some sea salt on the outside. Microwave it for 5 to 7 minutes. Serve with your choice of toppings (cheese, sour cream or plain yogurt, bacon bits, butter or butter substitute, etc.)

**2. TACOS.** Take a taco shell out of the package. Add a few scoops of canned chunky chili. Top with cheese (I like mozzarella on mine). Microwave for 1 to 2 minutes. Serve with salsa.

**3. RAMEN NOODLES.** You know what these are; they're the little "6 for $1" packages of noodles. You heat 2 cups of water until boiling, toss in the noodles, and they're ready in 3 minutes. Not too exciting. BUT – if you buy a bag of frozen Chinese vegetables and a bag of pre-cooked peeled shrimp, you can sauté these in a frying pan with a little hot pepper oil while the noodles are cooking. Toss them into the finished soup, and you've got a spicy oriental soup that makes a very enjoyable dinner.

**4. ALFREDO A LA QUICKIE.** My kids love this one: boil up a box of noodles – any kind – such as ziti, elbow, bowties. Sure, it takes 10 to 15 minutes to cook, but you only have to stir them once in a while. When they're done, drain, put into a bowl, and chop in a few chunks of butter (or butter substitute if you're watching your cholesterol.) Shake some powdered parmesan or romano cheese on top, add some pepper and salt, and you've got a quick cheesy meal. You could also sauté some meat or seafood if you'd like, and add that. It's fast, and it's very tasty.

**5. RICE WITH VEGGIES.** If you're constantly stretched for time, cook a pot of rice on Sunday and keep it in the fridge all week long. When you need to make a quick lunch or dinner, put 2 cups of the rice in a pot, add a little water, and heat on low for 5 minutes; it will be good as new. To top it, chop up a tomato, maybe some squash and carrots, whatever. (For convenience, you can also buy a bag of frozen veggies and use just a tiny portion. One bag will make about 5 or 6 dinners, so it's very cheap as well.) Sauté these with a little hot pepper oil until tender, then toss on top of the rice and add a little soy sauce. It's quick – it's tasty – and you'll think you ordered take out.

There are hundreds of these types of recipes out there. You'll get new ones every week by email if you subscribe to my membership site located at **www.grocerysavings.us**. Feel free to share your favorites with friends.

The secret to innovative, exciting cooking is to vary the sauces, seasonings and styles of the additional items you add to your core ingredients. As I mentioned above, most restaurant menu items are just a core ingredient with enhancements. So vary your enhancements, experiment, try new things, and you'll keep your menu vibrant and inviting. But first – you have to become an expert at cooking the core ingredients.

## Big Idea Recap – Chapter 14

**BIG IDEA 70:** *You really don't have to do a lot of fancy cooking to make good food when you start with nature's finest. It's hard to top perfection.*

**BIG IDEA 71:** *The food industry wants to DISCOURAGE you from cooking, so you'll buy their over-priced pre-mixed dinners. If you start building a list of quick, easy-to-cook recipes that use CORE INGREDIENTS and that your family enjoys, you can cut your food costs in half.*

**BIG IDEA 72:** *Wean yourself from the notion that cooking is difficult. Cooking can be one of the simplest things in your life, if you approach it correctly. It's the key to seriously reducing your food budget, too.*

**BIG IDEA 73:** *Cooking fast & delicious meals for yourself and your family should not be a chore. If it is, you're doing it wrong! Do it right, and you'll eat better, healthier food every day. Plus, you'll be saving LOTS of money.*

# Chapter 15: A System for Cooking = A System for Savings

### *How to Develop a System for Cooking Core Ingredients.*

If you're cooking-challenged, this chapter will be critical to your success in weaning yourself from pre-packaged meals. If you can really get the hang of cooking core ingredients, the rest is a cakewalk.

• If you can learn to make rice, you've got the basic foundation for about half a gazillion Chinese recipes. *(HINT: nature made this recipe easy. One cup of rice, two cups of water. It's always double the water for a single unit of rice; easy to remember.)*

• If you can learn to boil noodles, you can make Italian food with your hands tied. *(HINT: boil a pot of water. Set your timer to 10 minutes. Stir it once in a while. If they're still too hard at 10 minutes, cook 'em a few minutes more. Easy.)*

• If you can peel & boil potatoes, you can add countless varieties of toppings for a healthy, nutritious dinner. (Have you seen those 'potato martinis' they serve in the fanciest restaurants? They're nothing more than mashed potatoes topped with sautéed meats and vegetables. What a novel idea!) Once you determine how best to cook your core ingredients, the rest – pun fully intended – is gravy.

Get familiar with cooking core ingredients from scratch. Once you've got your own system down, the rest of the cooking process is a breeze.

**GOOD APPLIANCES CAN HELP.** We are so lucky today to have time-saving appliances available for every conceivable kitchen task. They can save you huge amounts of time in the kitchen, and many just about do all the work for you. So if you want to take control of your food budget and really cut your dependency on packaged meals, I would suggest that you take an inventory of your appliances. Investing in a few basic items could really make your life easier. This doesn't have to be expensive. Heck, the local pharmacy sells appliances now, and they frequently give $5 and $10 rebates for buying them.

Listed below are some items that I couldn't live without. Now, some of you nutritional purists will shudder at some of these suggestions. But hey, those of us on the front-line of the family-feeding war need all the help we can get. It's our job to keep the family happy, and if the family won't eat what we cook – what good is it? So cook what your family loves, and they'll love you back all the more.

**RICE COOKER.** One of the easiest things to cook is rice – and one of the best time-savers is to get a rice cooker. You dump your ingredients in, plug it in, and in 15 minutes or so your rice is done perfectly. You don't need to watch it, stir it or tend to it in any way. It's the ideal cooking helper, especially if you've got small kids to tend to. Plus, kids just love rice. And as a bonus – rice is still very reasonably priced. Buy a huge bag, and save.

**FOOD PROCESSOR** (or mini-processor if you're single or you've got a small family). Peel an onion, cut it into 4 pieces and drop it in the processor, press the "chop" button, and it's chopped in about 5 seconds. The same thing goes for carrots, garlic, scallions, squash – basically any hard vegetable. A good processor will cut your cooking time by half. And the bowl, blades & cover all go right into the dishwasher, so there's not a lot of clean-up. They're also ideal for grating hard cheeses. And let me share a secret that every fine Italian cook will tell you: buy a block of hard cheese and grate it in your mini-processor just before serving over your pasta. It will make an ordinary meal extraordinary.

**PRESSURE COOKER.** For some reason, these scare the daylights out of most people. They shouldn't – because a pressure cooker can cut your cooking time by 50% or more – and they lock all the nutrients into your food. Plus, a pressure cooker can make even the cheapest cuts of meat tender.

They're great for stews (cook for 15 minutes; turn off the heat and let it sit for 30 minutes, and your meat will fall off the fork.)

They make excellent chicken soup (put a chicken, vegetables, water and salt / pepper in the pot, once the pressure weight is rocking cook it for 20 minutes, cool for 30 minutes. It will be the best chicken soup you've ever had.)

They can cut an hour or more out of the cooking time required for meats such as pork chops. Just sear your chops in the pressure cooker in a little oil (adding garlic, salt & pepper for flavor) for about 3 minutes on each side. Add 3/4 cup water. Close the pressure cooker, turn up the heat, and cook for about 10 minutes once the weight starts rocking. Cool the cooker immediately and remove the chops. They'll be fully-cooked, tender and ready-to-eat. I like to remove them, top with bread crumbs, and brown in the broiler for about 3 minutes; it makes them look more appetizing and more like oven-baked chops. The only difference: you've saved at least an hour of cooking time!

They're ideal for cutting the time required to cook vegetables (cooks in 1 to 5 minutes after the pressure weight starts rocking; cool the cooker immediately with cold water, and your veggies are ready to serve.) Get over the fear; try pressure-cooking in your household and you'll be a convert for life.

**DEEP FRYER.** Yes, I know people want to live "healthy" and avoid fried foods. But what do the kids order every time you're in a restaurant? Heck, what do *you* order when you're in a restaurant? Being able to cook restaurant-quality fried foods in your household can significantly reduce your food budget. You just have to get over the 'guilt' factor and admit that most people love fried foods. Yes, it's a nutritional crime. But admit your vice and face your fears. It's not THAT bad for you from time to time… I bought a family-sized fryer at the drug store for $20 after rebate. It's really a great appliance. I can take a basic potato – probably costing about 25 cents or less – and create restaurant-quality fries in about 10 minutes.

Now, if you want to reduce the amount of fried foods you serve but still add the flavor and appeal of fried foods to your menu, try this. Make a pot of Japanese noodles – soba noodles are available in many import shops. Heat up some chicken broth for the soup. Chop up some vegetables – broccoli, cauliflower, carrots – and get some fresh peeled shrimp. Mix up some tempura batter, and deep fry the veggies and shrimp in the fryer. Serve over the soba noodles and soup and you've got a dynamic Japanese meal that the family will love. Plus, you've minimized the amount of fried foods you're serving. You see? A deep fryer is NOT the evil device you thought it was...!

**ELECTRIC GRIDDLE.** This appliance is indispensable in my household. The #1 use, of course, is to make pancakes. But it's also ideal for dozens of other recipes as well. One of my favorites is hash brown potatoes. Grate 3 or 4 potatoes in your food processor (SO much easier than grating by hand, and you don't skin your knuckles.) Grate an onion as well. Mix it all together with salt & pepper. Oil your griddle lightly. Spread the mixture all across your griddle and cook on medium-high heat for 15 minutes. Cut into 8 squares and flip each square and cook for another 10 minutes or so. The result is a flavorful, hearty breakfast or side dish. Total cost for 8 servings: about 15¢ a serving. The frozen hash browns in your grocer's freezer will cost about 3 times that amount, and the taste won't even come close to that of the home-made recipe.

## Big Idea Recap – Chapter 15

*BIG IDEA 74: Adding a few inexpensive appliances to your kitchen will make cooking easier, cheaper – and more nutritious for your family. Plus, it will help you switch to a "fresh cooked" diet rather than a "frozen / reheated" diet – which can save you big bucks on your groceries.*

# Chapter 16: Quick-Cooking: The Secret to Happier, Healthier Meals

Why do so few people cook fresh meals?  Do you give any credibility to these common myths:

- *I'm too busy to shop.*
- *There's no time to cook.*
- *I hate to cook.*
- *My family wouldn't know the difference anyway.*

Now, consider the alternative answers.

**– I'm too busy to shop.** You had enough time to buy the bag of pre-made stuff, didn't you?  Consider that you could buy a variety of core ingredients – many of which are also found in the freezer section – with just a few extra minutes of shopping time.

**– There's no time to cook.** Again, you're going to find enough time to get out a pan, add the glop, heat the glop and dish it up.  Plus, you'll probably find 20 or 30 minutes to eat the meal.  The moral of this story is this: you're already devoting a certain amount of time to meal preparation.  Consider some minor alterations to the ingredients you buy, the recipes you use (or don't use), and the way you prepare your meals.  Then, see if somewhere in your busy day you could find just 5 minutes to steal and re-apply to meal preparation.  The reward will be meals that can be much tastier and probably a lot healthier for you and your family.

If your schedule is SO TIGHT that you absolutely could not find 5 minutes anywhere – and your life is literally on a stopwatch every minute of the day – you probably have a personal shopper and a personal chef.  For everyone else, I'm pretty sure you can find the five minutes!

You can cook fresh meals from CORE INGREDIENTS in almost the same amount of time it takes to heat up a pre-mixed meal.  Consider some simple steps in the way you approach cooking, and you can save time, enjoy better meals, and lower your food costs.

**– I hate to cook.** This is a valid concern if you view cooking as a chore – which many people do. A lot of people choose DUMPING over COOKING, in the interest of saving time. To avoid cooking, many people simply DUMP bags or cans of glop into saucepans and heat it up. But I'd like to propose an alternative to cooking. What if you could just dump DIFFERENT bags or cans of stuff into the same pot, and enjoy it a whole lot more. I call this QUICK COOKING, and if you do it right it won't take you a lot of extra time. It <u>will</u> make your meals extra special, though.

Even if you DETEST setting foot in the kitchen, even if you find the recipe for boiling water too difficult, you CAN learn to cook quick fast, simple meals that your family will love. Take it one step at a time, and even the most die-hard mageirocophobiac (person with an intense fear of cooking) can become an efficient quick cooking expert and save money on food with a little patience.

**– My family wouldn't know the difference anyway.** You might be surprised on this one. The reason many families are oblivious to the taste or quality of their food is that they've never experienced real cooking. They eat what they're given, because it's all that they know. People eat bottled spaghetti sauce over pasta, because it's what they've always eaten; they don't expect anything better.

Look at the ingredients of the sauce: it's full of modified food starch, which is nothing more than a filler and it's aptly named. It FILLS you up but is it good for you? You can buy a can of crushed tomatoes for less than the can of prepared sauce; add a few pennies worth of spices, and make a much more satisfying and healthy meal.

The one and only ingredient in the can of tomatoes is TOMATOES. Don't you think that might be healthier than a ton of food starch and preservatives? YES! Do you think you might feel better by eating all-natural ingredients? YES! The proof is in the pudding (or pasta, in this case). Your family WILL notice the difference and chances are they'll thank you for the improvement. "QUICK COOKING" will allow you to produce quality meals for less, with almost no additional investment of your time. You end up taking the same basic steps you do now: open a can, rip open a bag, pull out a pan, turn on the stove. You're just being more selective in what you're putting into the pan, and how you're doing it. With just a few minutes of planning, you can make TREMENDOUS changes in the cost of your meals as well as your family's satisfaction with them.

Okay, how do we handle this "QUICK COOKING" without a lot of work and clean up? Let's look at a few core meal ingredients and how you can use them to create dozens of exciting, delicious recipes. For the sake of this discussion, it doesn't matter if you're a meat-eater or a vegetarian, a vegan or a Venutian; whatever you choose to cook, you can follow these tips and start cooking and eating better and cheaper.

## Insider Secret: You're Already Buying Core Ingredients – But Not At Their Source!

As previously mentioned, most cuisines – from the most basic to the most exotic – are variations on a theme. The chef (or food manager, in the case of packaged foods), starts with a core ingredient or multiple core ingredients. To these they add a variety of topping or add-ins to create the final meal that you eat. Here are some of the core ingredients that you can buy at the source as fresh ingredients, and the high-priced alternatives they replace.

| LOW-COST CORE INGREDIENT | HIGH-PRICED PREPARED ITEM |
|---|---|
| Rice - dry | Pre-cooked rice in frozen dinners |
| Potatoes - fresh potato wedges, etc. | Frozen French fries, dry potato flakes, frozen |
| Tomatoes - canned | Prepared spaghetti sauce |
| Fresh broccoli, beans, carrots, etc. - any fresh vegetable | Frozen or canned vegetables |
| Boneless, skinless chicken breasts | Tiny amounts of chicken found in prepared dinners |
| Pasta - uncooked | Canned noodle dinners or pasta mix meals |
| Oatmeal - large drum, uncooked | Tiny packets of partially-cooked dried oatmeal |
| Bread flour | Baked loaves of bread |
| Fresh meats, poultry and fish | Frozen, prepared meals with tiny portions |
| Baking Mix | Pre-baked biscuits, frozen or tube biscuit dough; frozen waffles |
| Homemade sauces & gravies | Cans or jars of sauce, or packets of dry gravy mix |
| Fresh tortillas, cheese, canned beans | Frozen Mexican food dinners |
| "Closeout" fresh vegetables (items that the store must sell today or throw away) | Vegetable soup in the can |

The secret to feeding your family well – with tasty and enticing food on a bargain-basement budget, with no time to cook and no time to shop – is in three key steps:

• **AVAILABILITY** of economical core ingredients; having them accessible.

• **FLEXIBILITY** to mix and match the ingredients that you can buy economically.

• **TECHNIQUE** to quickly prepare and cook your meals using some core sauces, seasonings and styles that are appropriate for your family's eating habits, (more about this later).

Think of food ingredients the way the chefs do: as building blocks to fine meals. Determine what you have to work with first (i.e. what's cheapest / freshest), then decide what you're going to build and how you're going to build it.

To get a handle on how remarkably simple these three steps can be, let's look at:
a. The way you buy these items.
b. The way you plan your menus.
c. The best way for YOU to cook, store, and serve nutritious meals your family will actually eat.

## Big Idea Recap – Chapter 16

*BIG IDEA 75: Regardless of how little or how much time you have to shop, train yourself to select CORE INGREDIENTS rather than pre-mixed meals, and you will save tremendous amounts of money.*

*BIG IDEA 76: You can cook fresh meals from CORE INGREDIENTS in almost the same amount of time as heating up a pre-mixed meal. Consider some simple steps in the way you approach cooking, and you can save time – enjoy better meals – and lower your food costs.*

*BIG IDEA 77: Even if you DETEST setting foot in the kitchen, even if you find the recipe for boiling water too difficult, you CAN learn to quick fast, simple meals that your family will love.*

**BIG IDEA 78:** *"QUICK COOKING" will allow you to produce quality meals for less, with almost no additional investment of your time.*

**BIG IDEA 79:** *Think of food ingredients the way the fine chefs do: as building blocks to fine meals. Determine what you have to work with first (i.e. what's cheapest / freshest), then decide what you're going to build and how you're going to build it.*

# Chapter 17: Planning Your Menus

*How to choose value ingredients to make luxury meals.*

Do you know how the world's greatest chefs decide their menus? Ask any chef what they will be cooking tonight, and they'll tell you that it depends on what is in season. Great chefs plan their menu when they go to the market. It may be the farmer's market, the fresh seafood market, or the wholesale meat market. If flounder is in abundance at the fish market and the price is lower than that of the other fish, tonight's special will be flounder. If shrimp is on sale, tonight's special will be shrimp.

You may wonder why the chefs use this method. Surely, they can charge whatever they'd like for the items in the restaurant? Well, technically they can. But that doesn't mean people will pay. Think of your own dining experiences. If the chef's special sounds appealing and it costs a few dollars less than the other items, don't you sometimes choose the special? Another reason to choose the chef's special is abundance. When an item is in abundance, it's often because the item is in season – and hence is very fresh and is available in large quantities. If the flounder is fresh and the other choices start out frozen, which do you think will taste better?

**CHEAPEST** can often mean **BEST** when it comes to food selections. That's because those items are in most abundant supply – and therefore the lowest in cost – are usually the freshest, because they are being harvested now – not six months ago.

## How to Cook Delicious, Nutritious Meals With Your Core Items

Let's review how a variety of core ingredients can be prepared, then enhanced with additional ingredients to create unique meals.

## RICE

Rice can be made from 'scratch' very easily. The fastest way is with a pressure cooker or a rice cooker. Nature came up with a very easy recipe for rice: 1 part rice; 2 parts water. Sounds pretty easy, huh? You may want to add a dash of sea salt, chicken bouillon, saffron or other spices, but it's usually best just to cook plain white rice. For families on the go, consider making a large pot of rice on Monday and using it in your recipes throughout the week. Just store the leftover rice in a plastic storage bowl. To reheat, just add a little water, cover and heat; nothing could be simpler. If your meals are more infrequent, i.e. you travel a lot and can't leave fresh food in the refrigerator, try freezing your rice in small plastic containers. You can 'nuke' rice back to health in your microwave, in a matter of minutes.

Make a large quantity of your core ingredients, and be ready to reheat them quickly for individual meals. You'll cut vast amounts of time out of your cooking procedures, and you'll eat fresh-cooked quality with every meal.

**Recipes.** There are countless ways to make tasty meals with rice. Some simple ideas are to add pre-cooked chicken, beef, sashimi (imitation crab), and vegetables. Let it steam for a few minutes. Add a splash of teriyaki, soy sauce, Worcestershire sauce, barbecue sauce or any other ingredients you like. For fried rice, simply heat some oil in a frying pan then add your rice and cook until slightly browned, then add your other ingredients. For egg fu yung, lightly beat one or two eggs in a bowl (but not so much that bubbles form), add to the rice mixture and flip after a minute or so. See? Cooking can be easy and fun!

## OATMEAL

Oatmeal has the same simple recipe, straight from nature: 1 part oatmeal; 2 parts water (or milk, if you like it richer.) Oatmeal is one of the only foods that actually cooks better in a microwave than it does on the stove. Try it; you'll be amazed at how smooth and creamy it comes out! For one serving, mix 1/2 cup oatmeal with 1 cup of water or milk. Microwave for about 3 minutes, then stir and cover with a plate to prevent splashing. Continue microwaving for 1 minute at a time until done.

# POTATOES

There are countless ways to cook with potatoes. Families existed on potatoes during the potato famine in Ireland, and they learned many different recipes to add variety. You can boil, bake, microwave or fry potatoes in many different ways; just get a good cookbook (at a yard sale or thrift store, of course...).

To prepare a base supply of potatoes early in the week, just peel and boil your potatoes until fully cooked. Then, store then in a plastic storage bowl until you need them. They'll only keep for a few days, so only cook what you can use fairly soon.

**Recipes:** Again, the possibilities for using potatoes in recipes are endless. Here are a few ideas, by meal:

**Breakfast:** Chop your cooked potatoes and fry them in butter to make tasty hash browns. Add a little cheese, hot sauce, chopped scallions, etc., for variety. Or, slice your potatoes and fry in butter to make home fries. Potatoes are an excellent addition to a hearty breakfast, especially at the start of a strenuous work day where you'll need extra energy.

**Lunch:** Poke some holes in an unpeeled potato and microwave it for about 5 minutes, and you've got a delicious baked potato that can serve as your main course. Add cheese, sour cream, bacon bits, cooked broccoli, etc., to make a tasty meal.

**Dinner:** Serve them baked, boiled & quartered with butter or chicken broth, mashed, etc. Use them as a 'base' with stew or sautéed veggies on top. Top with chili and cheese or canned meat to make a filling quick meal. Again, consult a recipe book and you'll be amazed at the uses for potatoes. The thing to bear in mind is that you can often find potatoes on sale for $2.00 or $2.50 for a 5-lb. bag. That works out to about 25 cents per potato – one of the cheapest, most nutritious foods in the grocery store. They're fat free, full of fiber, and tasty. If you're careful about what you put on them, they can be a healthy choice too. I suggest using the imitation butter spray and / or powdered and flavored 'butter buds' that are available today. These additives have almost no fat or calories, and can make a baked potato seem almost decadent even as this filling and flavorful meal actually helps you lose weight!

## TOMATOES

Why single out tomatoes as an ingredient? I'm also singling them out because they're the staple ingredient in Italian cooking, vegetarian cooking, and many ethnic foods from around the world. They're easy to grow and relatively cheap to buy – especially the canned variety. Yes, I know – you purists are saying you'd never eat a tomato out of a can. But for busy people they can be an excellent, fast alternative to fresh tomatoes – especially when you don't have time to shop, or you're frequently on the road and fresh tomatoes just go bad on the shelf.

**Recipes:** Get a cookbook to see any of the thousands of possibilities for tomatoes. Here are a few of my favorites:

**Breakfast.** Ever had a sliced tomato on the plate with your bacon & eggs? They're delicious anyway but you can add either salt or sugar for even more flavor. Chop them up and add them to an omelet or just eat a raw tomato with a little salt. In the summer, nothing is better than a fresh-picked tomato!

**Lunch.** Slice them and add to a ham or turkey sandwich. Try a home-made Bacon Lettuce Tomato sandwich (BLT). In the south, fried green tomatoes are also a delicacy.

**Dinner:** One of the easiest and fastest ways to make spaghetti sauce is to use a can of chopped or whole tomatoes. I like to sauté a little chopped garlic in olive oil, add the tomatoes and a little salt and pepper, and cook for 10 to 15 minutes. Pour on top of cooked pasta and you have a great Italian dish. You're eliminating all of the additives, starches and fillers that are common in the jars of sauce that most people use. Plus, cans of tomatoes are typically a lot cheaper than the jars of sauce. To quote Rodney Dangerfield, "Man – who don't like spaghetti?"

Tomatoes are packed with tons of nutrients and they have great natural flavor. They're one of nature's best sources of lycopene, a powerful antioxidant that may help your body's natural defenses prevent cancer, heart disease, and other serious diseases.

You can make hundreds of recipes using tomatoes as your base. I find that the less you cook tomatoes the better; the lighter the seasoning the better; and the sooner you cook the tomato after picking from the vine, the more taste it will have. Another tip: if you're ever at a farmer's market and you find heirloom tomatoes, buy them. Heirloom tomatoes are grown from seeds that are not currently in mass-production. There are hundreds if not thousands of varieties of tomatoes available, and many of these small-batch tomatoes – while not commercially feasible to grow – are loaded in flavor, unique taste and nutrients.

## VEGETABLES

Fresh veggies are probably the healthiest, tastiest items you can buy in a store. They're also probably one of the most misunderstood of foods. So many people would rather rip open a bag of frozen broccoli than deal with stalks of fresh broccoli – presumably because they 'want to save time'. Do you know the easiest way to cook fresh broccoli? Wash it off, put it in a glass or Pyrex dish, add a little water, cover with plastic wrap, strap a rubber band around the dish, put the dish in a microwave, then cook on high for about 4 or 5 minutes. You'll have perfectly steamed fresh broccoli that I GUARANTEE you will taste ten times better than the frozen stuff. The total time expenditure is about the same but buy the broccoli on sale, and you'll probably pay less. And guess what: this same approach works for asparagus, carrots, beets, potatoes; almost every vegetable out there…

Buy whatever veggies are on sale, fast cook as described above, and your family will begin to eat healthier, feel better, and enjoy meals more. Here are some tips to win over the anti-veggie contingent in your household:
• Spray some fat-free butter on the veggies before you nuke them. This is the 'zero calorie' spray that you find in the butter section. If you don't like this, try the powdered butter substitute found in the spice section of your grocery. Of course, you can always use regular

butter or margarine, but this will add useless calories and fat – especially the bad 'trans fats' – with little taste benefit. Even if you've avoided these low-fat products because they don't taste as good or work as well as butter on sandwiches or toast, try them on veggies and you will be pleasantly surprised.

• Use plain yogurt and butter spray on baked potatoes. You won't be weighed down with all of the fat of sour cream and butter but the potato will taste great. If you're a bacon lover, buy some of the dried bacon bits to sprinkle on as well.

   *- Tip 1: if the bacon bits are too hard on your teeth, nuke them in a small dish with a little water.*

   *- Tip 2: look for these in the discount spice rack at your neighborhood drug store. Normally, they're only 99¢ at the drug store, whereas the name-brand items can be $2-$3 at the grocery store.*

   *- Tip 3: Look for coupons for the spices in your Sunday paper. One major national drug store chain frequently issues coupons for spices at 3/$1. While most of their spices are about 95% salt, the bacon bits are a bargain, as are the chocolate and rainbow ice-cream sprinkles, especially when they're 3/$1. (Yes, I know the sprinkles are 100% refined sugar, but if you have kids you know that they go absolutely crazy for them and they're a big hit at birthday parties.)*

*Okay, back to veggies…*

• Buy close-out veggies when they are available at your store and make a healthy soup or stew out of them. The recipe is extremely simple:
   - Wash / peel / chop the veggies, as appropriate.
   - Put into a big pot, with some water and simple spices. (Hint: less is more when it comes to spicing up a veggie dish. Mother Nature put an immense amount of flavor and subtle tastes into veggies to begin with; you really don't have to add a lot more for most dishes).
   - Cook for about a half hour (or about 5 minutes if using a pressure cooker.)
   - Serve and enjoy. If you happen to find a LOT of veggies on sale, consider making a big pot of soup or stew and serving it all week

long, or freezing some for later. You can freeze soup in leftover plastic containers from yogurt, sour cream, margarine, etc. To reheat, simply pop the giant ice cube of soup into a pot and heat slowly for 10 or 15 minutes. Frozen soup or stew will keep for months, and taste just as good – and sometimes better – than the first time around.

Of course, you can buy full-price fresh veggies, and in most cases that is all you'll find available. But there is a special reward in making a giant pot of delectable fresh vegetable soup for $2 or $3. If you have a breadmaker machine and make a loaf of homemade bread for about 50¢, you can feed your family like royalty for less than $5 – and often enjoy 2 or 3 meals out of it, to boot!

• For a red sauce / French-style dish, add fresh or canned tomatoes prior to cooking.

• For a cream sauce, add a little milk, sour cream or plain yogurt near the end of the cooking cycle. To thicken, mix a little flour or corn starch with water in a cup, and stir the mixture into the broth slowly. *(Hint: do not add the flour directly to the mix, or it will turn to lumps and clumps of dough and powder. Be sure all of the flour is dissolved into solution BEFORE you add the mixture to the broth. Also, drizzle the mixture into the broth very slowly and keep stirring or the flour mixture can still turn into dough.)*

• For meat dishes, it's advisable to pre-sear the meat in a little olive or vegetable oil first. The meat can cook along with the veggies (allow extra time), but if you have cubed beef, pork or lamb, it just looks better when it's pre-seared.

• For a little European flair, add some white or red wine to the dish. The best time to do this is before you cook the food. Example: make some 'roux' in the pot before you start cooking the veggies or veggie / meat combo. A good recipe is to sauté some onions in butter until soft, then add some flour and spices to form a paste. SLOWLY add your wine to de-glaze the pan (all this means is that you loosen the sticky bits off the bottom of the pan and scrape everything into a consistent sauce). This roux / wine combination will thicken your sauce and add some very intricate and interesting flavors. Consult any good cookbook to find out which spices to use with which veggies or veggie / meat combination. You'll find that you can make some GREAT international dishes in no time at all if you learn a few basics such as this.

• For a totally mind-blowing culinary sensation, make a roux as described above and then when the dish is complete add sour cream, milk or yogurt to make a cream sauce out of your broth. Many Hungarian dishes such as goulash and Chicken Paprikash follow this process, and are among the tastiest meals you will ever eat.

• To stretch your soup / stew, cook some noodles separately and serve the soup over the noodles. You can make excellent fresh noodles using nothing more than flour and salt, or just buy pre-made noodles if you're short of time. You can also make a paste out of flour, water, salt and a little baking powder, and make excellent dumplings right in the soup, just prior to serving.

There is not a vegetable on this planet that cannot be cooked in hundreds of different ways, and in thousands of different combinations with different spices and sauces. The variety of dishes you can cook for your family is endless. 'Recipe boredom' does not have to be an issue in your household. You don't need a 'box mix' to add variety to your diet; you need a 'recipe mix' to shake things up, and excite your family's taste buds.

## DAIRY

Dairy is one area in which it can be difficult to cut costs – difficult but not impossible. Here are some tools and techniques:

**Cheese:** Buy blocks of cheese and grate them at home, rather than buying pre-grated cheese. Often, I'll find the small blocks of cheese on sale for about $1.00. The same amount by weight of grated cheese will often be $1.99 or more – literally double the price! Granted, if you don't have a food processor at home, hand-grating a full block of cheese will take a lot of effort. That is why I believe you should make every effort to get a food processor as soon as you can afford one – or get yours out of the attic and actually start using it. If you buy one bag of grated cheese per week for a full year, you've wasted almost as much money as it would take you to buy a food processor and grate it at home. How long does it take to grate cheese? It takes about 10 seconds, using a food processor with a grater blade. Then, you store the cheese in plastic container for future use. Another advantage of grating your own cheese is that you're not limited to American, Cheddar or Mozzarella; you can grate Monterrey Jack, Swiss, Colby, Sharp Cheddar or anything you'd like.

**Milk:** It's funny how milk prices can vary so dramatically by brand. Do the higher-price brands come from better breeds of cows? I don't think so. Always look for the lowest price brand when shopping. Another thing that amazes me at the store is how size-specific people have become. My local store regularly puts half gallons of milk on sale for $1.00 each, while a full gallon container will be priced at $2.79. Most people grab the gallon container out of habit. People: two halves DO make a whole when it comes to milk. Keep an open mind – and an open eye – when you're shopping for milk, and you can really save. And for you singles out there: never buy a pint of milk; you're paying about a 150% markup over the larger sizes. Buy a half-gallon or gallon, and freeze what you don't need in the short-run. Yes, milk freezes and thaws out just fine…

You can stock up on some FRESH items just like you stock up on canned goods. As long as you have a method of storing these items, you can buy them while they are on sale. Prices these days can change from week to week, so get the bargains whenever you can.

## MEATS

Most people avoid the lower-price cuts of meat, because they want their family to enjoy the finest quality. But here's a secret: all beef comes from a cow; all pork comes from a pig; all parts of a chicken come from a chicken. Sure, all the cuts are different and some cook up better than others, but many of the lesser-priced cuts can be turned into excellent, flavorful, enjoyable meals. It's all in the cooking process.

# Chicken

To fully understand how the different cuts and packaging combinations of chicken affect price, just look at the cost per pound of each variety. From lowest to highest price, here's what you're likely to find:

- Whole Chickens or 'fryers'
- Half or Quartered Chickens
- Specific-Section Packs, with all drumsticks, all wings, all bone-in breast sections, etc.
- Bone-in Chicken Sections, including drumsticks, breasts with wings attached, thigh sections, etc.
- Boneless Breasts - Skin on
- Boneless Breasts - Skinless / frozen
- Boneless Breasts - Skinless / fresh
- Pre-Seasoned Breasts or Tenderloins

Understand the 'preparation chain' of the food you buy. The higher up this chain you buy, the less you will pay; the lower down the chain you buy, the higher the price you pay. Often, the difference in the preparation time of your meals is just a few short minutes, or a few pennies worth of seasoning. But the difference in cost can be significant.

It would be easy to preach that you should always buy whole chickens and cut them up as needed, but this is simply not practical for many people. It's messy, it takes time, and it's not particularly easy unless you learn how to do it. What I DO recommend is staying as high up this list as possible, given the amount of time you can devote to cooking. I also recommend that you NEVER buy pre-seasoned meats, because you're paying a huge mark up for a few pennies' worth of spices. A relatively inexpensive and handy choice is skinless / frozen breasts, because they are there when you need them and they're easy to cook. Or, if you're willing to rebag them, you can buy packages of fresh breasts on sale, and freeze them individually for one-at-a-time use later.

Chicken can be cooked in a multitude of ways, so there is no great secret to buying individual cuts; just buy what you prefer, and look for the best value you can, based on how much cooking time and work you're willing to put in.

For example, I make a casserole-sized chicken potpie for fraction of the cost of buying a store-made pie. I simply cook two or three chicken breasts in the pressure cooker, and then I thicken the remaining liquid with a little milk and some flour and water paste to make a cream sauce. I add some carrots, onions, potatoes that I have cooked separately. Put this all into a casserole dish and top with a simple piecrust (takes just a minute to make with flour, salt and shortening), and bake for about 15 minutes. Start to finish takes about 30 to 45 minutes, and it will please a huge, hungry crowd.

## Beef

There are many different cuts of beef, and many ways to make tasty enjoyable meals using the lesser-priced cuts. Perhaps the best rule of thumb with non-ground cuts of beef is this: the cheaper the cut, the slower it needs to be cooked. Just about any cut of beef will come out tender and juicy if you slow cook it for about 3 hours at 250 degrees in the oven. You'll also get great results if you cook it all day in a crock-pot. My favorite way to cook lesser cuts of beef is in a pressure cooker. If you don't have a pressure cooker, you should definitely consider buying one – especially if you often find yourself short of time to cook.

With a pressure cooker, you can cook a delicious pot roast in less than 1 hour's time – start to finish. Try that in an oven – you can't do it! Here's the recipe:

1. Heat a little oil in the pressure cooker, and sear your roast on all sides for a minute or two.
2. Remove the roast and put the spacer in your pressure cooker. This is a little metal plate that keeps the food away from the direct heat; it comes with your pressure cooker.
3. Replace the roast, and surround with cleaned, peeled vegetables such as potatoes, carrots, celery, onions, etc. Use whatever is in season and/or on sale, which you like. You can add a can of tomatoes if you like a red sauce, or cut up some fresh tomatoes. I like to add chopped garlic, salt and pepper.

4. Add about 2 cups of water.

5. Close the cooker and heat until the weight starts to rock.

6. Cook for about 15 to 20 minutes.

7. Turn the heat off, but leave the cooker on the burner; let the pressure go down naturally.

8. The longer you let the pot sit, the more tender your beef will be. If you can, let the pot sit for an hour or longer, and you will have an incredibly tender roast. If you can't wait, you can place the cooker under running cold water to reduce the pressure immediately. If you are planning to cook and serve your roast immediately, I would recommend cutting the meat into smaller chunks prior to cooking. This way it will tenderize better.

You can cook ANY type of meat in a pressure cooker this way, and it will always come out great. If you want to serve your family hot, tasty home-cooked meals but find yourself challenged for time, I would strongly urge you to invest in a pressure cooker. They simply can't be beat as a kitchen helper.

Regarding chopped or ground beef, use your best dietary judgment rather than price to make shopping choices. The cheaper ground beef contains the most fat, which will be very evident when you cook it. If you do buy cheaper ground beef, drain it well after cooking. But remember – the value you thought you were getting will be going to waste when you drain away all the fat. And if you don't drain away all the fat, guess where it will be going? You may find that the costlier ground beef will yield bigger burgers with less fat, so they're actually a better buy in the long run...

Another way to tenderize cheaper cuts of beef is with meat tenderizer. The new types of tenderizer are NOT MSG-based, so there's no need to worry about your health. But they can make a world of difference in the tenderness of your beef; try it and see!

You can lower your meat costs by purchasing cheaper cuts of meat and cooking them differently. A little extra preparation time and changing your cooking methods can make these cuts of meat just as delicious as the higher-priced cuts.

# SAUCES: The Miracle Budget Stretcher

When you get right down to it, most meals consist of a base and a sauce. For meat-eaters, the core element is chicken, beef, pork or lamb, the secondary element is rice, potatoes or other vegetables, and the variable element is the sauce or other seasoning additive. For vegetarians, the core element is one or more vegetables, the secondary element is rice or other grains, and the variable element is the sauce or spices. That is why it is important to develop as many different sauce or spice combinations as possible. Once you've mastered these sauces, you can serve them over any core element to make delicious, healthy and flavorful meals.

Variety is the spice of life. If you family is bored with the food you cook, spice things up: simple variations on the sauces you use to top your food can make meals new & exciting again. And by using core ingredients as the base (rice, noodles, potatoes, etc.), you can keep your food costs low.

If you are typically stressed for time, you can actually prepare these sauces in large quantities and store them in the freezer. You can pour your cooled sauce into quart-sized heavy-duty plastic kitchen bags and freeze. Then, simply re-heat in a saucepan or in the microwave to serve. Or, if you're serving single portions, wash and save your leftover yogurt cups or pudding cups and freeze the sauce in them. Just put a sheet of plastic wrap or wax paper on top before freezing. With a little resourcefulness, you can work out your own system without buying expensive storage containers.

You could buy pre-made sauces, but they tend to be expensive and full of fillers and artificial ingredients. Here are some very simple, very tasty sauces that you can make in minutes. Serve them over your choice of core ingredients (cooked pasta, rice, meats, or vegetables) and create gourmet meals that your family will love.

**MARINARA SAUCE.** As mentioned earlier, commercial pasta sauces typically have a lot of starch fillers; you can make a better sauce that is 100% natural by buying diced or pureed tomatoes and adding a few spices to your liking. To make a delicious marinara sauce, fry some chopped garlic in a little olive oil. If you like, sauté some chopped onions or chopped green peppers as well. When they are transparent but not browned, add a can of tomatoes (or fresh, if available). Add a little Italian seasoning or basil (optional; I find that kids like it better without any spices), and heat for 15 to 30 minutes, stirring occasionally.

**CREAM SAUCE.** If you want a decadent meal that people will rave about, start with a small carton of heavy cream. Heat in a saucepan until it thickens slightly and then add your core ingredients. For example, you can add a can of peas on some chopped ham. Serve over hot noodles and sprinkle on grated cheese. This will taste WAY better than those 'quick side' pouch meals. Yes, it's high on the cholesterol and fat content, but if your goal is to impress, this will work every time.

**MUSHROOM SAUCE.** If your family likes mushrooms, you can make a great sauce by melting some butter in a saucepan (real butter is best for sauces, but margarine will do), adding mushrooms and a sprinkling of garlic powder or chopped garlic. Sautee for a few minutes and then serve over your core ingredients. Top with chopped chives for color, and you've got a great presentation.

**OLIVE OIL & GARLIC SAUCE.** This is known in Italy as "Aglio et Oglio" and it is a classic. Simply heat some olive oil in a saucepan and add chopped garlic (the jars of chopped garlic are easy and tasty; purists prefer chopping the garlic fresh, but it does take extra time…). Heat very briefly until garlic is barely cooked, then serve over cooked pasta. Top with grated cheese. The simplicity and powerful taste of this dish is amazing.

**BROWNED BUTTER SAUCE.** This dish has been served for thousands of years – literally. It is said that Homer lived on this dish while writing The Iliad, so you know it has to be good! Cook your noodles first, and when they're almost done, start on your sauce. Melt a stick of REAL butter (margarine will NOT work for this one) in a saucepan over medium high heat, stirring constantly. When the butter starts to burn, immediately take it off the stove, and pour it over your noodles. Top with grated hard cheese. You can use any really hard cheese such as Asiago, Parmesan, Pecorino, etc. (Grating a fresh block of hard cheese just prior to serving will make your dish much more flavorful than if you use the 'green cardboard shaker' cheese. I recommend getting a small electric chopper to save time – and save your knuckles.) The flavor of this dish will overwhelm you.

**YOGURT SAUCE.** A cool and refreshing alternative to oil-based sauces is a simple and clean yogurt sauce. Simply add some parsley, chopped chives and tarragon to plain yogurt, stir and store. For variety, add chopped cucumber (known as Raita in Indian cooking.)

**LEMON JUICE.** Squeeze fresh lemons into a bowl, remove the seeds, and serve on top of your favorite core ingredients. Nothing is lighter or cleaner than fresh lemon juice; it really brings out the flavor of vegetables. Try sprinkling on some fresh ground black pepper for extra zest.

**PESTO.** This one takes a little longer and a few more complex ingredients. Start with 3 to 4 cups of basil leaves, 2 to 4 cloves of garlic, a half cup of fresh parsley leaves, 1 cup shelled walnuts (optional), 1 tsp. salt and half cup of oil (preferably extra-virgin olive oil.) Puree in a food processor for a minute or two until smooth. Add additional oil until it forms a smooth paste. Add a half cup grated Italian cheese and process a few minutes longer until smooth. You can use Pesto to add zing to soups, stews and other recipes, or serve it on top of your core ingredients as the main sauce.

**SOUR CREAM SAUCE.** This is an elegant sauce that turns any core ingredient into a gourmet treat. Melt 2 tablespoons butter over medium heat in a saucepan, add 1 cup finely chopped green onions until transparent (but not brown.) Add 2/3 cup of whipping cream and cook until slightly thickened, stirring constantly. Reduce heat to low, add 2 teaspoons white vinegar, 2/3 cup sour cream and 1 teaspoon of salt. Heat through, but do not boil. This is an unusually pungent and tasty sauce, ideal for special occasions.

**WHITE MUSHROOM SAUCE.** Here's a quick and easy sauce that is sure to impress. Slice 1 lb. fresh mushrooms (try an egg slicer.) Saute' in a half cup of melted butter until golden. Stir in a half cup white wine, 2 tablespoons fresh chopped parsley, and add salt & pepper to taste. Cook for 10 min. on medium heat. Stir in 1 cup of heavy cream. Remove from heat immediately and serve over pasta, vegetables or any core item combination. Top with grated cheese.

**SPICY PEANUT SAUCE.** Up for something different? As Thai cooking grows in popularity, more people are discovering that spicy peanut sauce is great on barbecued meats, served as a dipping sauce, or just as a side sauce to flavor up any meal. Here's an easy way to make this sauce quickly. Heat a half cup of chunky peanut butter in a saucepan, stirring constantly. (I find that the fresh-ground peanut butter, typically found in health-food stores, is much better for cooking than the commercial brands. In a clutch, buy the all-natural jar of peanut butter; it will require stirring, but it's much better in the long run.) Stir in 1 clove of garlic, minced very fine. Add a dash of cayenne pepper, and gradually stir in a half cup of water and a half cup of canned coconut milk. Cook over low heat until the flavors are blended. Add salt and pepper to taste. This sauce is a bit exotic, but once you get a craving for it, it will be a welcome change of pace on your dinner table.

**ALMOND CREAM SAUCE** *(Korma, from India.)* Here's a decidedly elegant sauce you'll love as soon as you've tasted it. In India, they serve it over chicken and lamb, but it's also ideal just by itself over rice or with vegetables. Saute' 3 cups of finely chopped onions in 1 cup of olive oil (or clarified butter, but that takes extra work) over medium heat. Fry until wilted and pale brown, stirring constantly. Stir in 1 cup of slivered or ground almonds, 3 tsp. ground coriander, 2 tsp. chopped fresh ginger, 1 tsp. ground cardamom, 2 tsp. ground red pepper, 1 tsp. ground cumin and 1 to 1-1/2 ˌtsp. ground fennel. Cook for 5 minutes, stirring constantly. Remove from heat and puree in a blender with 2 cups of plain yogurt and a half cup of water. Add more water slowly until sauce is the right consistency. Pour back into sauce pan and cook until thickened. Add salt (course or sea-salt preferred) to taste. Remove from heat and cool at room temperature for 30 minutes or longer, then reheat prior to serving. (Flavors blend best when sauce is cooled then reheated.) Serve over barbecued, broiled or fried chicken, or your choice of core ingredient. Garnish your dish with fresh cilantro, if desired.

**HOT CHILI SAUCE.** If you like things on the hot side, you can make your own hot chili sauce in minutes. Simply mix the following in a saucepan: 3 tbl. Soy sauce, 1 tbs. Chinese black vinegar (or 1-1/2 tsp. Worcestershire sauce), 1 tbl. sugar, half tsp. hot chili paste, 1 tsp. minced ginger root and 2 tbl. warm water. Heat over medium heat for 5 minutes and serve over your favorite core ingredients.

**CHINESE IMPERIAL SAUCE.** How do the Chinese make so many different dishes so quickly? The secret is their base sauces. Here's one that you can make in advance and serve over just about any core ingredient to make a tasty change-of-pace dish. Blend the tastes, then store your cooled sauce in the refrigerator in a jar and heat in a saucepan prior to adding your core ingredients. Start with 3 tbl. Soy sauce, add 1 tbs dry sherry and a half cup chicken broth. Add 1 tsp. finely-chopped ginger, a half tsp. sugar, then salt, pepper and garlic powder to taste. Add a dash of MSG for flavor-enhancement, (optional; most people prefer no MSG.) In a small cup, mix 1 tsp. cornstarch with a little water to form a liquid paste. Drizzle slowly into sauce to thicken.

**CHINESE HOT SAUCE.** Here's another basic Chinese sauce that you can use to make a range of different menu items. In a small jar, mix 3/4 cup ketchup, a half tsp. bean sauce (found in Chinese grocery stores), 1 tbl. or more hot oil (see below), 3 tbl. Sesame oil and 1 tsp. of sugar. Mix until blended. Add chopped garlic, ginger, salt & pepper to taste, plus 1 cup or more of dry sherry to taste. To make hot oil, place a handful of dried red peppers in a jar and add oil (olive, vegetable, canola or any cooking oil you prefer.) When using, use the oil only and not the peppers. If you are cheap like me, buy the inexpensive bottles of red chili flakes at the drug store or 'dollar' store. They work great, and cost next to nothing!

**REMOULADE SAUCE.** The Cajuns in Louisiana use this sauce on all types of seafood and sandwiches. Mix 1 cup of mayonnaise with 1/8 cup Famous Sauce *(available at your store, name brand starts with a "D" and rhymes with turkey.)* Slowly add in 3 tblsp. olive oil and beat vigorously. Add 1 tsp. Creole or 'poupon' mustard and then mix again. Add 3 tsp. prepared horseradish, 3 tsp. ketchup, 1 tsp. Worcestershire sauce, 1 tsp. Louisiana hot sauce, beating after each ingredient. Add salt if desired. This is a spicy sauce that some people can't live without.

**MEUNIERE SAUCE.** This is also a Cajun recipe, ideal over seafood. In a small saucepan, combine 3/4 cup Butter or margarine, 3 tbsp. lemon juice, 1/4 tsp. salt, a dash of hot pepper sauce, 2 tsp. chopped green onions, 1 tblsp. minced parsley, 1/4 tsp. white pepper and a dash of Worcestershire sauce. Heat on low for 5 minutes until blended.

**ULTIMATE CREAM SAUCE.** For sheer elegance, nothing beats a complex cream sauce. This recipe uses ingredients you probably have around the house, and cooks very quickly. Melt a half stick butter in a saucepan. In a small cup, mix 2 tablespoons flour with a little hot water until dissolved. Blend the flour mixture into the melted butter until thickened. Add a half cup hot milk and slowly blend in 1 pint sour cream. Bring to a simmer. Add 1 can cream of mushroom soup and a half cup hot water. Whisk until blended. Blend in 2 tsp. grated parmesan cheese and allow to melt. Bring to a simmer and then add 6 oz. dry white wine. Add 1 tsp. white pepper and 1/8 tsp. each of cayenne pepper, dried oregano and dried thyme. Simmer until thickened. Pour over any core ingredient for a delightful meal.

As you can see, the variety of sauces you can cook is unlimited. These are but a few of the many, many sauce recipes you can find in your favorite cookbooks or on the Internet. Add to your list of sauces, and you will find that you can create exciting and varied dishes in minutes – for meals that your family will savor and thank you for again and again!

## Big Idea Recap – Chapter 17

*BIG IDEA 80: CHEAPEST can often mean BEST when it comes to food selections. That's because the items that are in most abundant supply – and therefore the lowest in cost – are usually the freshest, because they are being harvested now – not 6 months ago.*
*BIG IDEA 81: Make a large quantity of your core ingredients, and store them in a way that you can reheat them quickly for individual meals. You'll cut vast*

amounts of time out of your cooking procedures, and you'll eat fresh-cooked quality with every meal.

**BIG IDEA 82:** *A large bag of potatoes has more nutrition, more food volume, and more value than just about any item in your grocery store. The Irish knew this centuries ago, and that is why it is the mainstay of their diet.*

**BIG IDEA 83:** *Tomatoes are packed with nutritional value and flavor. You can make hundreds of recipes around the tomato, and each will be tasty and healthy for your family to eat. That is why the Italians have been able to make thousands of individual recipes based off of this one vegetable.*

**BIG IDEA 84:** *There is not a vegetable on this planet that cannot be cooked hundreds of different ways, and in thousands of different combinations with different spices and sauces. The variety of dishes you can cook for your family are endless, so 'recipe boredom' does not have to be an issue in your household. You don't need a 'box mix' to add variety to your diet; you need a 'recipe mix' to shake things up, and excite your family's taste buds.*

**BIG IDEA 85:** *You can stock up on some FRESH items just like you stock up on canned goods; as long as you have a method of storing these items, you need to buy them while they are on sale. Prices these days can change from week to week, so get the bargains whenever you can.*

**BIG IDEA 86:** *Understand the 'preparation chain' of the foods you buy. The higher up this chain that you buy, the less you will pay; the lower down the chain that you buy, the higher the price you will pay. Often, the difference in the preparation time of your meals is just a few short minutes, or a few pennies worth of seasoning. But the difference in cost can be significant.*

**BIG IDEA 87:** *You can lower your meat costs by purchasing cheaper cuts of meat and cooking them differently. A little extra preparation time and changing your cooking methods can make these cuts of meat just as delicious as the higher-priced cuts.*

**BIG IDEA 88:** *Variety is the spice of life. If your family is bored with the food you cook, spice things up: simple variations on the sauces you use to top your food can make meals new & exciting again. And by using core ingredients as the base (rice, noodles, potatoes, etc.), you can keep your food costs low.*

# Chapter 18: Miscellaneous Cost Cutters

Here are some random tips for saving money at the grocery store.

## DRINKS

• Brand-name soft drinks by the can are expensive. Choose the store-brand, or if you just don't like them, buy the quart, liter or 2-liter sizes of the brand-name stuff, and serve in a glass with ice. Your money will go a lot farther!

• Iced tea by the can or by the jar of mixture can be expensive. Tea bags are cheap! You can make fresh-brewed tea in the microwave in minutes and then add ice cubes and sweetener to make your own tea for less.

• Kids love slushees, but they cost $1.50, $2.00 or more at the burger joints. You can make them at home using a blender, some ice, and some pre-sweetened packet drink mix. We use the sugar-free varieties, because the kids get less 'wired' than with the sugar mixes. You can also use this method to make summertime adult beverages – mix in a little fresh fruit and lemon or lime as well, and you can make a great daiquiri without paying for those high-priced frozen mixes.

• Fruit juice is very healthy and delicious, but it can also be very expensive. Compare the cost of a half gallon of fresh orange juice to a can of frozen juice that makes a half gallon. It can often be almost 50% less in cost – and some frozen brands taste just as good as fresh, especially if you whip the concentrate with water in a blender. It really opens up the taste. And in many cases, that container of 'fresh' juice is actually factory-blended out of "FOJC", as it's known on the commodities market (Fresh Orange Juice Concentrate.)

What is at the core of any non-alcoholic drink? Water. Avoid buying drinks that have the water added at the factory, and replace it with clean & fresh water out of your own tap. You'll avoid a huge mark-up, and you'll lower the volume and weight of groceries that you have to truck back to your house.

## COOKIES & SNACKS

• The store brands of cookies are often as good if not better than the name brands. Plus, they cost about half as much.

• If you give your kids snacks for school, use your own plastic bags and dish out a small portion of these items from a larger bag. Those small pre-packs of snacks are about three to four times more expensive, by weight, than bagging the same portion yourself!

## PORTION CONTROL

The marketing gurus at the food manufacturing companies have latched onto a great idea: package smaller amounts of their product in tiny packets, and double or triple the cost of the item by weight. Market it as 'healthier-size portions' and people will pay the mark-up and be glad for it. AVOID THESE PRODUCTS, because you're paying a wildly-inflated cost for the food inside those packets. If you want to implement portion control, buy the large-size package and divvy the product out into small baggies yourself. You'll accomplish the same goal, but lower your total food bill.

If you are super-diligent about this, you can purchase one of those food-saver machines. You know, the ones that use a roll of plastic pouch material; you cut off a section of pouch material, melt one edge to seal it in the machine, fill it with your food, and then the machine sucks out the air and seals the flap air-tight? They're really not that expensive to purchase. Now, here's the advantage. Let's say that your kids just absolutely love those chocolate-coated candies, but they're very expensive – and the kids will overeat them if you buy the large economy size. With one of these machines, you can individually package your own portions and lock them up in a storage closet. The net result: one 5 lb. purchase can last for a full month, but instead of spending $20 or more on individual packets, you've spent $6 plus another $2 or $3 in plastic supplies. Does it make a difference? Well, if it's an item you buy every month, you're saving $133 or more per year – and best of all you're keeping the little ones happy, because they haven't had to make any sacrifice.

# CLEANING SUPPLIES

• One thing will never change; the need to clean. So when you're buying household items like laundry detergent, dishwasher soap, etc., buy the big container and use a coupon; this stuff won't go bad, and by buying big you won't be running out as often.

• **Shop at the dollar stores.** You'll find a treasure-trove of cleaning supplies at the dollar store for the remarkable price of... you guessed it – a dollar! And the remarkable thing is, many of these items will actually be environmenally-friendly. I found a huge bottle of orange spray cleaner – you know, the kind that uses citric acid as the main cleaning ingredient – and it only cost $1. This same type of product, when purchased at the "oh so environmenally conscious" earth-friendly store will cost you as much as $4.79! So you're reducing your cost by over 75% by purchasing at the cheapskate store. Does it somehow make you feel cheap? It shouldn't. It should make you feel **smarter.**

• **Read the 'Hints from Heloise' column** in your newspaper, or log onto one of the many websites that show you how to make clone-copies of brand-name cleaning products yourself. Many of these items such as window-washing solution, oven cleaner, bathroom cleaner, etc., can be made out of a combination of water, rubbing alcohol, vinegar, baking soda, ammonia, etc. – saving you 70% to 80% off the cost of buying the brand-name stuff. Just do a web search on "homemade cleaning supplies" and you'll find dozens of sites offering recipes for cleaners that you can make for a fraction of the cost of the name-brand versions.

You'll find that many of the home-made products will actually be better for your home and for the environment. For example, one web site lists a recipe for furniture polish that is made entirely out of olive oil and lemon juice. They claim that most commercial polishes and sprays use silicone oil, which can seep into the cracks in the wood and cause problems if you ever decide to refinish the wood. Their home-made version works just as well as the commercial stuff because the lemon juice dissolves the dirt and smudges on the surface while the olive oil shines and protects the wood. Imagine that – a cheap and effective product that does a better job than the high-priced sprays! Make your own cleaning solutions and you can easily save $20 or $30 per month off your grocery bill. Many of these home-made products actually work better than the store brands as well.

## SUPER BARGAINS

• Often you will find that your store is discontinuing an item, and will put it on sale for pennies on the dollar to clear it out quickly. When you see bargains like this, consider buying a few extras for the less fortunate. Every town and city has a center that accepts food and household items for the poor, and they will certainly appreciate your thoughtfulness. And if you happen to find pet food or pet supplies on close-out, buy a bunch of everything and drive it out to the animal shelter or ASPCA. Our furry friends need help, too – and their caretakers never get enough money or support to provide the animals with everything that's needed. And that brings up another very important point: saving money to help **others**.

### Help Your Community with Coupons – Even If You Won't Personally Benefit.

There are many people who could benefit from your shopping activities. One of the best and largest grocery-related programs around is "Boxtops for Education" sponsored by General Mills. It helps local schools get free or discounted educational supplies, based on the number of coupons that the school turns in for credit. With this program, you simply clip the little coupon that is printed on the packaging and collect them. Each one is worth about 10 cents towards school supplies or educational equipment.

Since General Mills is such a large manufacturer and distributor of food products, you'll find these coupons on dozens of different products you buy every week. The program costs you nothing extra, but the proceeds that your local schools can receive from it are huge. Just keep a plastic bag in your pantry or kitchen drawer and clip these coupons all year long – even if you don't have school-age kids. You could collect enough over one year's time to provide $20 or $30 worth of educational supplies for your local schools. Helping to provide a better education for our children is something we can all be proud of.

Of course, there are many other community groups that could benefit from the discounts and bargains you are able to achieve through proper shopping techniques. One immediate idea is to see if you have a Second Harvest or other food bank in your area. Food banks collect canned goods and non-perishable items for distribution to hungry families throughout your area. When you do see an incredible bargain on a particular item, you can be a hero by purchasing one or two extra items and donating them to the food bank.

## QUALITY

• It needs to be said that nothing substitutes for good quality. If you see a clear-cut difference in the quality of an item, and the higher-priced item is definitely of better quality, chances are the item is well worth the price they are asking for. Value is not as important as providing the best quality for your family so price should not be your only motivation when shopping. If you follow the methods outlined in this book, you can enjoy the finest items in the store for a fraction of the everyday retail price. But if you find yourself buying inferior products just to save a few pennies, what's the point? Life is too short, and you and your family are too important to settle for second best. Rather than sacrifice quality, I would recommend buying a smaller portion of the better quality items and consuming less. It will be more enjoyable in the long run.

If you find yourself buying inferior products or lowering your standards in the quality of the food you buy, you're not using the system correctly. It's easy to enjoy BETTER food and pay LESS money if you follow the steps outlined in this book. Spending less money on food does NOT mean you have to buy lower quality items.

## Big Idea Recap – Chapter 18

*BIG IDEA 89: Cut down on drinks that have water added at the factory. Buy concentrated juices and powdered drinks. You'll avoid a huge mark-up, and you'll lower the volume and weight of groceries that you have to truck back to your house.*

**BIG IDEA 90:**  *If you want to provide portion-controlled servings, consider buying the large economy-size package of a product and doling out the portions yourself. You can use plastic bags, or if you are especially resourceful, get a food-saver machine and make air-tight pouches for long-term use.*

**BIG IDEA 91:**  *Make your own cleaning solutions and you can easily shave $20 or $30 per month off your grocery bill. Many of these home-made products can actually work better than the name brands!*

**BIG IDEA 92:**  *Quality of life is important, and therefore the quality of the products you purchase and use is also important. Use the tips in this book to buy top-quality products for less. Saving money does NOT have to equate to settling for less.*

**BIG IDEA 93:**  *Be an "angel" and participate in free programs such as "Boxtops for Education" that help others. Or simply buy extra non-perishable items when you see them on super-sale and donate them to your local foodbank. You'll help out your community and store up some good karma while you're at it.*

# Chapter 19: Online Coupon Hunting

If you have access to the Internet, you can get some great coupons online. Plus, if you find a coupon for a product your family uses a lot, you can print off as many as you like.

Use the internet to your advantage BEFORE you go food shopping. If you need a coupon for peanut butter, run a web search for "Peanut Butter Coupon". You'll find dozens – if not HUNDREDS – of coupons that you can print immediately. Repeat this for all of the other main products you will be shopping for. A half-hour spent searching for coupons can easily reap $20 - $30 or more in savings. It's like having a part-time job that pays you $40 or $50 an hour, only you're not working: you're having fun.

## Value – with a Cost.

You should be aware that many of these 'free coupon' sites are really consumer survey / information-gathering portals for the food manufacturing industry. The site will ask you a wide range of personal questions about your household, and your answers will become part of a compiled database file on the members of your household.

One site promises that your data remains safe, and will not be shared with third party firms. But if you read their Privacy Policy, there are so many loopholes and 'trusted partners' who get your information, it is clear that you are being profiled every step of the way. Be wary, and if you are concerned about privacy and "Big Brother" knowing too much about you and your family, do not participate in their surveys, and provide the minimum amount of answers required to get to the coupons on their site.

**Here is a trick:** if you are required to answer questions about your usage of a product prior to your printing the coupon, always skew your answers in the direction the marketers are looking for. For instance, one offer I came across was for chocolate powder that kids use to flavor their milk. The website asked for two answers prior to receiving the coupon:

1. How many times per week does your household use milk flavorings?

2. How many of these instances involved the brand name featured in the coupon?

I answered the maximum in each case, and I was quickly routed to a 'technical malfunction' page that said the coupon could not be printed at this time. Why do you suppose that would happen? Answer: they didn't want to cannibalize their profits from a current customer. So when you encounter these 'surveys', ALWAYS say that you are interested in the featured product and would like to try it, but you currently use a competing brand. This way, you are almost certain to get the maximum value coupon available on the site that day.

**Here's another trick:** Some of these online sites will ask you to enter your Zip Code to find "local savings." I discovered something surprising about this. It's actually a ploy they use to REMOVE the coupons for items that are already on local promotion in your area.

How do I know this? Recently, two of my local stores had a name-brand line of potato mixes on BOGO. These are the box mixes of augratin or scalloped potatoes. Because the same offer was made at the two largest grocery chains, it was apparent that this was a major push to get people to try these products at the start of the fall/winter "hot food" season. I went to my favorite online coupon site and saw a 40¢ coupon for this item on page 1 of the site. Just to see what would happen, I entered my Zip Code to get the local offers, and the potato coupon disappeared from the list. I thought it was an error, so I logged out and logged back in again. Guess what? No potato coupon was found!

Just out of curiosity (and frantic to get my potato coupon) I logged in using a different browser (Internet Explorer instead of Firefox) so there would be no 'cookies' stored for my account, *(techie note only; ignore this if you find it confusing.)* I logged in using a Zip Code from another state, and guess what – the potato coupon reappeared!

Now, I tend to be cynical, but it sure appeared to me that the food manufacturer didn't want me using both the doubled coupon AND the BOGO offer. Here's why:

| Normal price of item | $1.29 per box |
|---|---|
| Cost per item using only the BOGO offer | $0.65 ($1.29 total for 2 boxes) |
| Cost per item using BOGO offer AND the doubled coupon | $0.25 ($1.29 minus $0.80 for 2 boxes) |

Of course, the internet coupon was marked "Do Not Double". But I know from experience that most stores ignore this request because they want to please the customer; they'll typically double every coupon that is within their accepted value range (any coupon under 50¢ at my local store.)

Moral of the story: you may want to avoid asking for "local savings" coupons if you really want to save more money locally.

Here are some coupon sites to visit, and some tips on getting the best coupon values on each site.

**CoolSavings.com.** This site features about 20 to 30 coupons per week on all types of consumer products. Just be aware that they are partnered with dozens of information-compiling sites, and unless you uncheck the requests on their pages, you will instantly be signed up for a wide array of offers. Read the fine print carefully and uncheck all offers before proceeding, or you will forever be inundated with emails and marketing offers.

**Eversave.com.** This site will make you work hard to get to the coupons – but it's worth the effort. On a recent visit, I was asked to review and "accept" or "skip" about 8 lengthy offers for insurance, medicine, magazines, etc. But then the payoff was huge: 82 coupons were available to pick and choose. The easiest way to do this is to "select all" and print. They even put the coupons in the same position on each page, so you can cut a stack of pages all at once and the coupons will all be trimmed out correctly!

**OnlineCoupons.com.** This site offers pre-clipped coupons, and you get to choose by specific brand names. There is a $99.95 annual fee however, so you should be a very avid coupon user to cover the start-up fee.

**Thecouponclippers.com.** Here, you don't pay an annual fee, but you do pay for each coupon. Fees typically range from 5¢ to 15¢, plus a 50¢ administration fee. One annoying thing about this site is that on coupons that cost you 5¢, the shopping cart changes the quantity to 5 – even if you only selected 1. But overall, this site has a huge selection of coupons at very reasonable prices. Plus, you don't have to do all that clipping…

**Clipngocoupons.com.** On this site, you have to agree to complete a very lengthy survey and tell them everything about yourself – in great detail. You have to go through quite a bit of mumbo-jumbo before you ever get to the coupons.

**Coupons.com.** This site requires you to register with minimal information, plus you must install their printer drivers to print coupons. They offer a large number of coupons at very good price points, on items that your family is very likely to want and use – items like popular cereal brands, gourmet food items, personal and cleaning products and more. A good site to visit often! NOTE: this site is re-branded by local newspapers such as the L.A. Times, the Baltimore Sun, etc., so you will be directed here from many other sites.

**CentsOff.com.** This site requires that you pay a $7.50 fee to join, then pay an additional $8.25 to receive up to 50 coupons by return mail. You select the coupons online and receive them in the mail within 7 to 10 business days. This site is well organized; it displays the specific coupons available by category, as well as the number of coupons currently available and the expiration date. You can order multiples of the same coupon, so if your family is a big consumer of a particular item, you can stock up on the specific coupon. Plus, you can plan your savings over time, up until the expiration date of the coupon. The drawback is that you have to pay to save, and that just kind of goes against the grain of true cheapskates. I would recommend this site if you are buying for a community group such as your Boy Scout

Troop or church social group, when you plan to make multiple purchases of specific items over the long term.

**MyClipper.com.** This site uses a double opt-in validation process. It means that you sign up on line and then you receive an email that you must respond to if you want to get to the online coupons. You are required to provide specific household information to sign up. The site features a surprising number of local coupons that you can print out and redeem for discounts on dining, shopping, entertainment, etc. I was impressed at the high coupon values and diversity of local establishments participating on this site. There are no grocery coupons on this site, however. The site simply links to EverSave.com for grocery discounts, so it may be disappointing if you are looking for printable grocery coupons.

**Thefrugalshopper.com.** This site maintains a large number of links to coupon values, many leading to the sites listed above, but also some unique freestanding sites great for rebate-searching, too!

**Fatwallet.com.** This is a great site for sharing coupon tips and techniques with people from across the country. You'll find 'hot deals' on coupons, rebates and regional offers posted here, with comments from people who have claimed them or have comments about the offer. Members of this site post information about hot deals and web sites where you can download coupons. Plus, they provide valuable information about what offers are good and not so good. The food industry giants monitor this site, because you will regularly find responses from the PR departments of the big companies, especially when a consumer posts a complaint here. As posted on their site, "FatWallet's mission is to serve consumers with knowledge, value and guidance. It's like having 230,000 friends to ask advice from, and all the rebates and coupons to make it happen at the lowest possible price."

**GroceryDiscounts.us.** This is the author's web site, so I really can't toot my own horn. But visit it, and see what you think. We offer many links to the best savings of the week. Plus, you can get valuable tips from hundreds of other value-conscious shoppers across the U.S. You are not the only consumer that wants to save money on groceries.

Millions of people today have to count pennies to stay afloat. You can benefit from their experiences and wisdom by searching the internet and reading about their tips & techniques. Knowledge = cash savings for you. Join some of the 'blogs' (web logs) related to cost-cutting, and share your successes with other value-minded individuals.

## Big Idea Recap – Chapter 19

*BIG IDEA 94:* *Use the internet to your advantage BEFORE you go food shopping. You'll find dozens – if not HUNDREDS – of coupons that you can print and redeem immediately.*

*BIG IDEA 95:* *Use the internet to capture tips & techniques from other shoppers. Chances are, you'll learn some great money-saving tips that you can use over and over again. Plus, you might just meet a kindred spirit on one of the blog sites, and make a new friend.*

# Chapter 20: Grocery Store Etiquette

One thing to bear in mind as you implement these saving techniques we've discussed, is that you're definitely going to be spending more time at your local grocery store. Okay, you might only be spending a little more time than you do already, but you're going to get to know your local store pretty well, one way or another. This certainly brings us to the issue of your fellow shoppers.

People's behavior in the grocery store is a mirror reflection of their attitude towards others. It was Honore De Balzac who said, "Courtesy is only a thin veneer on the general selfishness." Unfortunately you'll find this to be the case among the people sharing the aisles of your grocery store. You can't teach a stranger what their mama was unable to many years ago. But you can demonstrate proper courtesy yourself and hope that some of it wears off on others.

Here are a few ways you can become a more courteous shopper and make everyone's shopping experience more pleasant.

**Cart Courtesy.** When you're not moving, pull your cart over to the side of the aisle so others may pass. Nothing is more frustrating that waiting behind someone who is stopped in the middle of the aisle, and either doesn't know – or doesn't care – that other people are shopping in the store at the same time.

Similarly, if you're waiting in line at the butcher or deli counter, be aware of where you left your cart. If it's in the middle of the aisle and you'll be waiting in line for 5 minutes or longer, you'll probably be blocking a few dozen shoppers during that time. Take a minute to think of other shoppers, and pull your cart off to the side before you get in the line.

**Shelf Surfing.** If you're taking a particularly long time to review the products on the shelf, take a glance around every so often to see if anyone is waiting nearby. As it often goes with Murphy's Law, two or more people will need the exact same item on the exact same shelf at the exact same time. So if you see someone lurking nearby, they're probably waiting for you to move. So make your choice and move on.

**Cashier Courtesy.** It's important to mention that the cashier at your local grocery store is working to feed his or her family. They're not there to represent the 'big bad grocery store chain' or 'big corporate food manufacturers.' They're just people, like you and me, trying to make it through their shift. So give them a break. If you have a discrepancy on a price, don't jump down their throat: mention that there is an issue with the price that the scanner has entered.

Instead of, *"hey – you're trying to rip me off!"*, try, *"oh oh – I think the scanner took the original price and not the sale price. Can we check the sale flyer to see if I've got the right item?"* In other words, put the blame on the computer and not on the poor cashier who is just doing his or her job. It makes for a more pleasant exchange. Plus, the cashier is NOT trying to rip you off; she's there to help you, and she wants your shopping visit to be pleasant. Plus, it reflects poorly on her if she's got a situation with an irate customer. So give her a break, okay?

**Wrong Price / Wrong Coupon.** If there is a huge line at your grocery store and the scanner simply won't ring up the correct price or accept your coupon, don't pitch a fit or blame the cashier: offer to fix it at the Customer Service counter *after* you check out. If you're certain that you are entitled to the lower price or the coupon redemption, take it up with a customer service representative after you finish paying for your groceries. Your fellow shoppers will be very appreciative, as will your cashier.

Here's another value-shopping tip for you: most stores have a 'no error' policy that will give you one of the sale item FREE if their system rings up the wrong price. So your 5-minute excursion to the service counter could save you a few extra dollars, as well... And, needless to say (but I'm going to say it anyway,) if you're wrong, you can accept your error, apologize, and simply walk away from the service counter. But if you try to resolve the situation in the checkout line and hold the other shoppers up for 5 minutes or so, they'll never let you live it down. Plus, the cashiers will have you pegged as a 'problem customer' which is not a good way to make friends or get preferential treatment when you shop.

# Big Idea Recap – Chapter 20

**BIG IDEA 96:** *If you notice a price discrepancy at the cash register, it can pay to NOT mention it to cashier. Instead, walk over to the customer service counter after you've paid. You may get one item free if the pricing error was caused by the store's computer.*

# Chapter 21: Miscellaneous Time-Saving / Money-Saving Tips

Here are some ways to save time at the grocery store, at the same time you are saving money using the tips and techniques found in this book.

**Free & BOGO Coupon Presentment Order.** A cashier recently told me something about the processing of 'free' and 'BOGO' coupons. There are many coupons that offer an item for free but they also indicate that the cashier must write the purchase price on the coupon. The cashier asked me to always hand them the coupon at the same time they are scanning the free item, so they don't have to search for the price. A good tip is to put those items LAST on the conveyor belt, and put the free and BOGO coupons FIRST on your stack of coupons. This makes it easier for the cashier to find the prices. They'll really appreciate your effort!

**Competitive Price-Matching.** One of America's largest discounters offers a unique value proposition. Let's call them store "W" and affectionately nickname them "Wally World." This particular store will match their competitor's advertised sale price on the exact same item. This information can be used to your advantage in many ways.

Let's say, for example, that store "A" has put the large size of laundry detergent on sale, regular price $7.99 but this week it's on sale for $3.99. This may be one of the only loss-leaders they advertise for the week. Store "A" has the goal of getting you to come in for that one bargain, but purchase the rest of your weekly food needs at their regular store prices. If you take store "A's" flyer to store "W", you can purchase this same item for $3.99 – all the while taking advantage of store "W's" other low prices.

But the fun – and the savings – don't have to end there. You can also take flyers from store "B" and from store "C" and "D" into store "W". In other words, you can get the price-saving advantage of shopping at ALL of the stores in your are, but you won't have to burn up your valuable time and gasoline to visit these stores. This one tip alone can shave $20 or $30 off your weekly food bill. The bad news is, many stores like store "W" do not double your coupon's value. Now, I'm not suggesting that you ONLY buy the price-match items at store "W." That wouldn't be fair to them. And honestly, many times the net cost of items at store "W" are lower with single-value redemption on coupons that they are at competing stores with double-value redemption. You'll just have to do the math yourself to decide which stores in your area offer the best final-cost pricing on the items you need.

**Speed Shopping.** If you only need three or four items to complete your meal on a Sunday afternoon, you probably want to breeze in and breeze out of the grocery store. You're probably a wiz at the 'self-scan' aisle and know how to shave minutes off your trip. All this is great, but it can be very costly if you don't time to shop for bargains or take advantage of the in-store sales on that particular day. The secret to accomplishing BOTH of these goals is to do a little pre-planning.

You're in a huge rush at 4 p.m. when you need those three or four items. But you're relaxed and taking your time at 8 a.m. when you're reading the Sunday paper. I find it very beneficial to scan the grocery flyer from my local store. I locate the sale items, and then I do a quick perusal of my grocery coupon envelopes to see if I have matching coupons. I pull out the coupons and place them in the envelope I've got named specifically for that store, i.e. "Acme Grocery". I may find only three or four coupons, but when I'm breezing in to Acme for my 10-minute kamikaze shopping blitz, I run by and pick up those three or four sale items that I have coupons for. It only takes an extra two or three minutes to pick them up, but they are the best bargains for that day in that store. The net result: I experience savings of 40% or 50% on my total order that day, when I would have otherwise experienced savings of probably 0% had I not taken the extra few minutes to scarf up these values.

**Make Saving a Habit.** Paying full retail for food is a bad habit, and it's one that 90% of all shoppers fall into. Most of the time, they don't know any other way. If you habitually follow even a few of these money-saving tips, you will save money on food. In time, you will consistently find yourself paying less for food because you have changed the way you shop.

**Never Settle for Poor Quality.** Once in a blue moon, you will purchase an item that will either have gone bad, taste horrible, or just not be usable. If it's defective, return it to the store for a new one; the grocers expect a certain amount of 'breakage' as it's known in the trade. If the item is in fine condition but you just think it's nasty-tasting, write a quick letter to the manufacturer and tell them so. I recently bought a juice item for my kids, and they all spit it out. Even their friend who weighs 300 lbs and regularly cleans out my refrigerator of all leftovers, he spit it out. So I wrote a note to the manufacturer and told them that they needed to reformulate or at least re-think the product, because my personal focus group is pretty reliable when it comes to evaluating kid's foods. The manufacturer wrote me back and send me three $1.00 off coupons for their other products. So it was well worth my time to complain.

**Grow Your Own Vegetables and Herbs.** Okay, I know what you're thinking: I barely have time to zip through the grocery store. Now you're asking me to put on bib overalls and farm the back 40? What are you, CRAZY??? No, actually, it's nothing like that. If you have a patio or deck, or even just a few square feet on the side of your driveway, you can grow your own tomatoes or green beans and save lots of money on fresh vegetables.

Tomatoes grow very well in a large bucket – and you can often find the large 5-gallon plastic pails thrown away behind restaurants or in the recycling bin. (Is that unethical, to take things out of the recycling bin? No! You are doing better than recycling – you are re-using!) If you like gourmet cooking, nothing is better than fresh basil, thyme, cilantro, parsley, etc. – and these grow very well in small pots that you can put on a window sill. Try it. You might be surprised at how easy it is to grow your own herbs and save on the cost of buying them fresh.

**Start a Soup Night.** Every grocery store has vegetables that are reaching their peak and must be sold quickly. Turn this to your advantage, and use them to make a pot of soup! Mondays are good days for grocery stores to clear out their leftover inventory from the weekend. So if you pick up a bag of mixed vegetables for $1 or $2, you can cook them up in a pressure cooker and make a delicious soup in less than an hour. You can also find meat that is expiring and on-sale for half the price or less, that is still absolutely fresh and good to eat that day but must be sold by the store before midnight to comply with basic regulations. Take advantage and cook it all up together with a few spices. It makes a terrific dinner. Bake a loaf of fresh bread the night before, using your breadmaker, and you have a gourmet treat that's easy on the budget as well.

## Big Idea Recap – Chapter 21

*BIG IDEA 97: Some big-box grocers offer to match competitive store's sales prices. By taking the other store's sales flyers into the big-box store, you can enjoy the best values from every store in your area, without the added cost or time of actually driving to all of these stores.*

*BIG IDEA 98: If you get in the habit of ALWAYS picking up a bargain or two EVERY TIME you visit the grocery store, you will see a consistent and ongoing reduction in your net cost of food. If you make bargain-grabbing a habit, you will habitually save on food.*

*BIG IDEA 99: You never have to pay for items that truly are unusable. If they're defective, get your money back or get a replacement. If they're just poorly made or you are completely dissatisfied with them, write letters: you'll get satisfaction in the end – and probably save a few extra bucks as well.*

*BIG IDEA 100: A few minutes per day invested in growing your own vegetables and herbs can easily save you $20 or $30 per month. That's up to $360 savings per year – plus you'll eat better and tastier meals.*

*BIG IDEA 101: Bargain meats and vegetables are still very edible and nutritious; the store couldn't sell them if they weren't. By learning how to prepare these items quickly, you can not only save money – you can prepare them into a delicious, welcome meal that your family will love and look forward to every week.*

# Closing Notes

Well, there you have it. I hope that the ideas presented here have given you a new outlook on food and cooking in general. You don't have to settle for second best, and you don't have to pay top dollar to get the finest groceries available in the store. You can shop quickly and efficiently, regardless of how time-challenged you are. You can feed your family for less and enjoy nutritious, delicious meals that can improve their health and you can save lots of money in the process.

Good shopping to you all. May your coupon-cutting scissors remain sharp, and your piggybanks remain full!

# GLOSSARY

Guide to refunding and couponing terms :

Blinkies - instore smartsource coupon dispensed near product, usually from red blinking box
BOGO or B1G1 - Buy one get one free
Catalina - coupon dispensed at register after purchase, usually has a red border
C/O - cents off coupon
Codes - Refunds that require only a UPC# written on a CRT
Coufund - for coupons that need some proof of purchase such as UPC's attached
Cpns - manufacturer's coupons
CRT - Cash register tape
DCRT- Dated cash register tape
DCRTC - Dated cash register tape with the price circled
DND - Do Not Double (the coupon is not supposed to be doubled)
Double coupon - coupon that a grocery store doubles in value
Free Item Coupon - A coupon that allows you to get the product completely free
FSI - Free Standing inserts. These are the actual term to the coupons you get in your Sunday newspaper. Also referred to as SS coupons or insert coupons.
HBA - The health and beauty aid section in the grocery store
HDA - Hot Deal Alert or Home Delivered Ad
HT or HgT- Hang tags for refunds or coupons hanging on a product
HTH - Hope this helps
ISO - In search of
LTD - Limited, as on a refund form it will say you're limited to a certain number of purchases
MFG - Manufacturer
MFR - Manufacturer
Money + - Premiums that require money in addition to a proof of purchase
NAZ - Name, address, zip code
NB - National Brand
NBQ - National Brand Qualifier

NED - No expiration date
Nfp - refund form found in a newspaper
NT WT - net weight
OAS - a coupon that is good on one purchase, any size
OSI - On a single item
POP - proof of purchase
PP - purchase price
PPHF - Paypal handling fee
Q or Qualifier- The POP required for a refund offer that is physically taken from that package
RAOK - Random act of kindness
SF - Store form
SMP - specially marked packages
SS - Sunday supplement coupons (FSI)
Super doubles - coupons that are doubled $1 + in value (ie, a $1 coupon = $2, etc)
SWEEPS - sweepstakes form
Tear pad - A pad of refund forms found hanging from a store shelf or display
TMF - Try Me Free
Triple coupon - a coupon that a grocery store triples in value
UPC - Universal Product Code
WSL - while supplies last
YMMV - Your Mileage May Vary (Success of offer is variable.)

# Savings Example

**Total Before Savings:** $128.35
**Total After Savings:** $87.47
**Total Savings %:** 31%

# Savings Example

```
Balance Due                    42.62
   Credit     Purchase         42.62
- - - - - - - - - - - - - - - - - - -
   PRESTO!
   Reference #: 057093-003
   Trace #: 0010015991
   Acct #: XXXXXXXXXXXXX2664
   Purchase MasterCard
   Amount: $42.62
   Auth #: 467825
- - - - - - - - - - - - - - - - - - -
   Regular Tax                 -0.05
   Food Tax                     3.30
   Total Tax                    3.25
   Change                       0.00

Your Total Savings
   Store Coupon                 2.56
   Advertised Special Savings  21.20
   Advantage Buy Savings        0.66
   Your Savings at Publix      24.44
```

**Total Before Savings:** $67.30
**Total After Savings:** $42.62
**Total Savings %:** 36%

# Savings Example

Publix
Cool Springs Pla (615) 221-5800
Store Manager: Joe Zaroscie

| | |
|---|---|
| SUBTOTAL | 120.19 |
| Regular Tax | 3.56 |
| Food Tax | 7.29 |
| ORDER TOTAL | 131.04 |
| Credit   Payment | 131.04 |

PRESTO!
Reference #: 057125-003
Trace #: 0010011761
Acct #: XXXXXXXXXXXXX2864
Purchase MasterCard
Amount: $131.04
Auth #: 658490

| Change | 0.00 |
|---|---|

Your Total Savings
| | |
|---|---|
| Store Coupon | 6.08 |
| Vendor Coupon | 12.30 |
| Advertised Special Savings | 64.95 |
| Advantage Buy Savings | 1.24 |
| Your Savings at Publix | 84.57 |
| Partners      41888305700 | |

**Total Before Savings:** $215.61
**Total After Savings:** $131.04
**Total Savings %:** 39%

# Savings Example

**Publix**
Cool Springs Pha (615) 221-9860
Store Manager: Joe Zarcone

(itemized grocery list, largely illegible)

| | |
|---|---|
| SUBTOTAL | 109.39 |
| Regular Tax | 1.66 |
| Food Tax | 8.18 |
| ORDER TOTAL | 119.23 |
| Balance Due | 119.23 |
| Credit    Payment | 119.23 |

- - - - - - - - - - - - - - - -

PRESTO!
Reference #: 051747-003
Trace #: 0010012391
Acct #: XXXXXXXXXXXX2664
Purchase MasterCard
Amount: $119.23
Auth #: 970572

- - - - - - - - - - - - - - - -

| | |
|---|---|
| Change | 0.00 |

**Your Total Savings**

| | |
|---|---|
| Store Coupon | 7.03 |
| Vendor Coupon | 9.43 |
| Advertised Special Savings | 50.68 |
| Advantage Buy Savings | 3.62 |
| Your Savings at Publix | 70.76 |

**Total Before Savings:** $189.99
**Total After Savings:** $119.23
**Total Savings %:** 37%

# Savings Example

Publix

```
Publix

Duc Savings Pre (813) 221-9890
Store Manager: Joe Carlone

AR ORIG MEATBALLS           2.99 † F
AR ORIG MEATBALLS           2.99 † F
PUBLIX FROZEN YOGRT
1 @  2 FOR    6.00          3.00 † F
    Adv Buy Savings  0.43
PUBLIX FROZEN YOGRT
1 @  2 FOR    6.00          3.00 † F
    Adv Buy Savings  0.43
BOTTOM ROUND STEAK          1.79 † F
    Ad Spec Savings  0.79
BOTTOM ROUND STEAK          1.76 † F
    Ad Spec Savings  0.79
BOTTOM ROUND STEAK          1.82 † F
    Ad Spec Savings  0.79
PUB LC CUT CHEESE           2.09 † F
PUBLIX MILK                 3.59 † F
PUBLIX MILK                 3.59 † F
LOR SLCD HNY HAM            2.99 † F
    Ad Spec Savings  1.00
YOPLT YOGURT
1 @ 10 FOR    6.00          0.60 † F
    Ad Spec Savings  0.15
YOPLAIT YOGURT
1 @ 10 FOR    6.00          0.60 † F
    Ad Spec Savings  0.15
DJ N/CAL FLA NAT
1 @  2 FOR    6.00          3.00 † F
    Ad Spec Savings  2.89
YOPLAIT YOGURT
1 @ 10 FOR    6.00          0.60 † F
    Ad Spec Savings  0.15
YOPLAIT YOGURT
1 @ 10 FOR    6.00          0.60 † F
    Ad Spec Savings  0.15
YOP FR VAN YOGURT
1 @ 10 FOR    6.00          0.60 † F
    Ad Spec Savings  0.15
YOP ...
1 @ 10 FOR    6.00          0.60 † F
    Ad Spec Savings  0.15
PRO LT VEG NOODLE
1 @  1 FOR    6.00          1.20 † F
    Ad Spec Savings  0.39
PRO STAL WEDDING
1 @  5 FOR    6.00          1.20 † F
    Ad Spec Savings  0.39
CLASSICO VODKA SCE
1 @  2 FOR    2.69          1.35 † F
    Ad Spec Savings  1.34
CLASSICO ONION/GAR
1 @  2 FOR    2.69          1.34 † F
    Ad Spec Savings  1.34
BB SWEET PEAS
1 @  4 FOR ...
```

| | |
|---|---|
| Balance Due | 171.22 |
| SUBTOTAL | 157.40 |
| Regular Tax | 2.75 |
| Food Tax | 11.67 |
| ORDER TOTAL | 1 .2 |
| Credit      Payment | 171.22 |

PRESTO!
Reference #: 055841-004
Trace #: 0010018511
Acct #: XXXXXXXXXXXXX2864
Purchase MasterCard
Amount: $171.22
Auth #: 218007

| | |
|---|---|
| Change | 0.00 |

Your Total Savings

| | |
|---|---|
| Store Coupon | 6.18 |
| Vendor Coupon | 15.12 |
| Advertised Special Savings | 53.96 |
| Advantage Buy Savings | 5.44 |
| **Your Savings at Publix** | 80.70 |
| Partners       41888305700 | |

**Total Before Savings:  $251.92**
**Total After Savings:    $171.22**
**Total Savings %:        32%**

# Savings Example

**Total Before Savings:** $119.68
**Total After Savings:** $68.52
**Total Savings %:** 42%

# Savings Example

```
          TAX                        9.52
    **** BALANCE               126.54
    ***********2864
 REF#: 217601
          Credit               126.54
          CHANGE                 0.00
 TN 07.7500 % TAX A              9.47
 9.25 State City N/F Tax         0.05
 TOTAL TAX                       9.52
 TOTAL NUMBER OF ITEMS SOLD =     60

 *********** KROGER SAVINGS ***********
 MFG CPN SAVINGS            $    5.65
 BONUS CPN SAVINGS          $    2.35
 KROGER PLUS SAVINGS        $   43.02
 TOTAL SAVINGS (30 pct.)    $   51.02
 *********** KROGER SAVINGS ***********
```

```
      *SEE WHAT YOU ARE SAVING TODAY*

 YOU SAVED $45.37
 WITH YOUR PLUS CARD

 ANNUAL KROGER PLUS SAVINGS $107.57

    THANK YOU FOR SHOPPING KROGER
```

**Total Before Savings:** **$177.56**
**Total After Savings:** **$126.54**
**Total Savings %:** **29%**

# Savings Example

```
**** 9.25% TN SALES TAX           .48
**** 7.75% TN SALES TAX          9.41
**** BALANCE DUE               127.30
VF     MASTERCARD              127.30
***********************************
MASTERCARD              $$$$$$127.30
ACCOUNT #  *****************2864
REF #       677008
EFT SEQ #   1773
CARD WAS SWIPED AT PINPAD
***********************************

          CHANGE                  .00

        COUPONS TENDERED 72.26
3/16/08   3:54 PM 0193 08 0051 704

   ** YOU SAVED57.96 ON THIS ORDER **
PRESENT YOUR VIC CARD WITH EVERY ORDER
   TO RECEIVE PROMOTIONAL DISCOUNTS!
```

**Total Before Savings:** $185.26
**Total After Savings:** $127.30
**Total Savings %:** 31%

**Total Before Savings: $234.64**
**Total After Savings: $134.79**
**Total Savings %: 43%**

LaVergne, TN USA
24 May 2010
183782LV00003B/10/P

9 780977 710607